TRUE STORY OF
BAROUMBAYES JOURNEY
—— FROM ——
AFRICA TO UNITED STATES

NOUBAISSEM BAROUMBAYE

Copyright © 2022 Noubaissem Baroumbaye.

All rights reserved. No part of this book may be reproduced, stored, or transmitted by any means—whether auditory, graphic, mechanical, or electronic—without written permission of both publisher and author, except in the case of brief excerpts used in critical articles and reviews. Unauthorized reproduction of any part of this work is illegal and is punishable by law.

ISBN: 979-8-88640-511-8 (sc)
ISBN: 979-8-88640-512-5 (hc)
ISBN: 979-8-88640-513-2 (e)

Because of the dynamic nature of the Internet, any web addresses or links contained in this book may have changed since publication and may no longer be valid. The views expressed in this work are solely those of the author and do not necessarily reflect the views of the publisher, and the publisher hereby disclaims any responsibility for them.

One Galleria Blvd., Suite 1900, Metairie, LA 70001
1-888-421-2397

CONTENTS

Foreword v

Acknowledgments vii

Introduction ix

The Family I Was Born into and My Education 1

Next Adventure in the Capital N'Djamena 24

Another Wind of Adventure Begins to Blow 40

Culture Shock 76

Job Search and First Permanent Job 80

Beginning of Life in Gunnison 91

The Family's Trip from Chad to Gunnison, Colorado 107

References 133

About the Author 135

FOREWORD

It is time to write a commemorative biography of my life. After a long delay influenced by procrastination, it is finally time to recap the key points of my purely exceptional journey. There are visions or projects that come from an individual; for example, traveling, getting married, writing a book, and so forth. I am not a writer, and writing a book was not part of my dreams. Since I was in the United States of America, many people have been curious about my motives for leaving my family and my country, and coming to another continent. Every time I finished telling my testimony, almost one in three people who listened to me said, "Nouba, you have to write a book." I was not paying attention to that proposal. The main cause was being very busy pursuing studies while working full time or partially at different periods. The goal that has just been achieved, which is becoming a licensed practical nurse (LPN), has given me the opportunity to work three or four days and benefited many days of rest. The thought of realizing the dream proposed by people who were interested in my life had awakened in me. This is to confirm the saying "Better late than never."

ACKNOWLEDGMENTS

Special thanks to my wife, Florence.

My children Sephora, Kelita, Mathilde, Daniel, and Grace.

My nephew Ramadje, his family, and his parents.

My parents, brothers, and sisters.

My extended family and friends in Chad.

My friends in the United States of America.

My church leaders in Chad, Cameroon, and the USA.

All the glory be to my miracle working God.

INTRODUCTION

I will start talking at length about my family and my basic education. I will also expand to talk about my academic career, which was not very famous. You will understand my weaknesses and the way I chose my wife, who remains my wrestling companion for about twenty-five years. I will certainly detail my adventures, which started from Goundi in the southern part of Chad. The stages in my career and the work of God are also interesting and filled with testimonies. So is my stay in Cameroon for theological studies. The last phase of the adventure is the life in the United States, which started from February 10, 2008, until now. Not 100 percent of readers of these pages will be excited, but certainly, a few will be proud that their lives were better and different than mine. I will pray to God that at least they will give thanks to him for the better life. Other men or women will regret not waiting a little bit longer to achieve their goal or save their marital relationship. I would like that many will rejoice in the particularity of each person and the grace that will follow each one of us. I wish you will not be bored reading my book.

THE FAMILY I WAS BORN INTO AND MY EDUCATION

I am originally a Chadian by nationality. My father was monogamous. Are you wondering why I mentioned this? It is because polygamy is allowed in Chad. I had eight siblings, but death took back a sister and two brothers.

My father had died in 2009, but my mother is still alive and remains in the family residence. My father was initially a farmer, but the wind of rural exodus brought him to the city, then an opportunity allowed him to travel to Gabon. After two years, from there, he was told that if he did not return, his fiancée would marry another man. His bosses had asked him to go back, get married, and come back to Gabon; but he had declined the contract offer and had returned to his country permanently. He had the chance to get the woman of his choice back. They settled in the southern province of Chad called Fort Archambault, which had become Sarh due to the future change of names of the provinces initiated by the first president of Chad N'Garta Tombalbaye.

Let us talk a little bit about this town of Sarh. It was considered the fourth major city of Chad after N'Djamena, the capital; Moundou; and Abéché. Apart from the administrative areas, the city had no electricity, no drinking water, and no official physical addresses. The houses are built of *poto-poto*, which is earth kneaded in mud to build directly or molded into bricks before making the construction.

My dad, having been trained in the field of masonry during his adventure, had maintained this profession for a long time. Chad has different seasons, one of which is the rainy season. The family did farm because the products for the harvest were used as surplus food instead of buying everything at the market. A few years before his death, my dad had returned as a full-time farmer because he felt in danger by continuing the masonry due to his age.

Who were my parents? Martin Baroumbaye (a father, Christian, and hardworking man who wanted the success of all his children) and Cécile Baroumbaye (a mother, Christian, and someone who makes every effort to never see her children sleep hungry). Both parents had not gone to school, but they wanted us children to succeed in school even if they were disappointed in one way or another. I was born on November 7, 1963, in the city of Sarh. Being the third child who was the first boy following two older sisters, I had received much paternal than maternal advice. Dad used to say to us, "I sent you all to school. It's the responsibility of each and every one of you to study hard and to succeed. If you did not work the fields when you were young and if on the day of difficulty first you would decide to try, the earth would cut your skin like a sharp knife."

As he learned the Sango language of the Central African Republic, my father would make me sit down in the evening to read the Bible in Sango, and he would translate it into our native Sara language so that

I also understood, for I had not learned Sango like him. Getting used to these practices of reading the Bible at home and going to church, for me, I considered myself a Christian. It was at the time of civil war between Christians and Muslims. I asked my father that in case I died during this troubled period, would I go to heaven? He said no. I asked him why, and he said, "You must make Jesus your Lord and Savior first. You would be saved."

Neither he nor I had thought of leading into the immediate confession. I had planned to do so on the Sunday that followed. After the worship service, I had spoken to the leaders of the church (Jonas Toningar, Marc Ranebaye, and Samuel Tradoumngar), who were excited to lead me into the confession of my sins and had prayed for me. These leaders have all died. May their souls rest in peace.

Returning to the series of advice sometimes, he said that if a young person were rich and spoke among the elderly and a poor old man spoke at the same time, one person in the group would say to this old talker: "Shut up so that we can listen to what the young person has to say to us." What was the point of this? It was to tell me to work hard and to have financial or material means despite my age. I would be respected in society. That was his point of view, but by reading the Bible a little more, I discovered that King David's point of view was better: "Oh, how I love your law! I meditate on it all day long. Your commands make me wiser than my enemies, for they are ever with me. I have more understanding than the elders, for I obey your precepts" (Psalm 119:97–100). He also said that a village chief who would travel to other places would serve his people and foreigners better than another chief who was born and raised in the same village without going anywhere. I understood this word of wisdom in different context in this country. I thought it was his pride because he had traveled out of Chad. Since my immigration to the United States, my contacts with people who have been outside of the States or those who have met foreigners in universities or through marriage had tolerant attitudes. I was talking about tolerance in the field of foreigner's color or language with an accent. In Leviticus 19:33–34,

God gave advice to the Israelites: "And if a stranger dwells with you in your land, you shall not mistreat him. The stranger who dwells among you shall be to you as one born among, and you shall love him as yourself, for you were strangers in the land of Egypt: I am the Lord your God" (NKJV).

The advice did not stop there. He also said that in a home, the wife herself could control herself and remain faithful to the husband. When you, husband, went to work, the wife could do whatever she wanted on the way to the market or clandestinely at home. Speaking of women, he added that a woman of exceptional complexion or beauty could not change the nature of the man who went to bed with her. It was Dad's way of warning against fornication and, later, adultery once being married. His advice on fidelity was lifesaving for us who respected it because some of my brothers had fallen into the trap of several concubines and AIDS.

He advised us about cigarettes and alcoholic beverages by saying that once tested and especially when done in a repetitive way, it would be easy to become addicted and it would be hard to quit. Proverbs 20:1 says, "Wine is mocker. Strong drink is brawler, and whoever is led astray by it is not wise" (NKJV). Advice that does not penetrate deeply into the heart has harmful consequences. They will still save if we remember and use them.

During my teenage years, Dad saw me rubbing shoulders with the girls in the neighborhood, and he told me to be careful because school was like a woman, and taking a girl was both hard and difficult responsibilities to manage. When I was sixteen years old, the temptation grew in me. One night, unluckily, my mother saw a girl in my room, and she informed my father.

Dad called me and said, "My son, if a family were ever to force you to marry their daughter, you would take at least one that would be beautiful and hardworking but not the one your mother would have seen in your room."

Fortunately, nothing had happened between us because I understood later that it was a trap. If I were trapped that day, it must have been a disappointment for my family and a prominent suspension for my studies because my dad would put me out of the house to take care of the girl by myself.

Bad company corrupts morals, as the Bible says. A friend with whom we always played and went to church invited me to join his father in local liquor store. The first few times, I drank only a small amount, but over time, I overflowed the doses. Unfortunately, I could not hold back, and I was throwing up. My dad was mad, and he seriously yelled at me. His reproaches stopped me for a while, but the desires came back later. I had also failed in the sexual field, but I had risen and decided to remain vigilant so as not to fall again. The apostle Paul said in Romans 7:15, "I do not understand what I do. For what I want to do I do not do, but what I hate I do" (NKJV).

Later, being away for a training that I will talk about later, I had fallen into the second temptation of my life; immediately, I had asked the girl to accompany me to my pastor. To her surprise, I had confessed my sin of fornication with her before the pastor and the elder. They told me what Jesus had told the adulterous woman in John 8:11, "Neither do I condemn you, go and sin no more" (NKJV). What a humiliation for her but what a victory for me. This life of victory had lasted for a few years. The long term of bachelor life made me fall once again with different girl; I had not delayed confessing to another servant without the girl this time. As I sincerely wanted to serve God without compromise, I had decided to marry, and I had remained faithful to God and my wife despite other forms of temptations that would arise because of long absences that occurred later in my life.

The word of God, like this, helped me a lot: "Therefore bear fruits worthy of repentance" (Luke 3:8 NKJV). Refusing to fall and getting up every time was a necessary decision for me. Living on the path of falling and asking for forgiveness, as Proverbs 24:16 says, "For a righteous man may fall seven times and rise again, but the wicked shall fall by calamity," may end because I have had dangerous experiences.

Experiences were the reality of sudden death that explained life is too short and never play with it. Four times I was going to die: In the first situation, I was pursued by an armed soldier. In the second situation, I was arrested by a group of soldiers in the same year. You would ask yourself the question, for what cause? The answer would be without cause. These were the years in which president Hissene Habre was in power, and the soldiers rejoiced in killing for pleasure. The third situation was a truck accident that almost took my life, but shouting in the name of Jesus for help had saved my life; the proof was that the driver, his apprentice, and eight passengers had died in that accident. In the fourth situation, I had slipped from a cliff, headfirst toward the valley; once again, shouting to Jesus for help reversed the tragedy. Finally, only my right kneecap was broken, not my neck. I had recovered several months later when I regained my mobility. I had remembered the advice on addiction (drink, cigarette, and sex), and I had repented once and for all. I have rarely been snagged by my parents. My mom was not the last to correct her children. When she saw a trash left by someone, she would insist until the person cleaned it up as quickly as possible. I have adopted this behavior: I hate dirt for the rest of my life. Every evening, she would send us to pick up the stems or twigs to light the fire.

A so-called education that I did not want to touch, but a lot of people, upon seeing the scars on my face, asked me what it was. I told them that this was the initiation I had had to undergo at the age of eleven with the other men and boys for a few months in the bush. Westerners who understood certain African cultures said it was the transition from childhood to manhood.

To return to the characters and habits of my father, he liked to sing and he was always present at home if he was not busy somewhere. He had a spiritual gift; his dreams were always achievable. I inherited the domain of singing during work time and the side of having true dreams.

Dad was always an early bird in the morning; either he would go to his workplace or he would do something at home early in the morning. His tea was always ready before sunrise. Surprisingly, one morning, he had not left his room. You would wonder how my mom would not know where he was. The parents, according to the tradition, slept in separate rooms. I woke up a little late that day. I had not seen him outside. Without asking any member of the family who was without concern for dad's absence, I had opened his door, which was not blocked inside. He was lying there, and I was asking him what was wrong as he was still in bed so late.

He said, "Thank you, my son. I decided not to go out today to find out if one day, I would die, one of you would find my body as quick as possible and that I would not be rotten alone in my room. Now I wouldn't worry anymore."

He had blessed me that day, and I had come out of his room without sharing with anyone what had happened.

I took all this time from you without saying anything about myself. Please excuse me for putting you on hold. You must know that it is important that you know my origin and my basic education that made me who I am today. Before talking about my life, you must understand that many individuals have contributed in one way or another. It would have taken me a long time to contact each one of them to get their permission to write their names in my book. The smart way would be for me to write only the initials of their names. I will mention them anyway, but if they will be angry when they see their names, I will ask them to forgive me. Some people also might think that I have violated their privacy by even posting their pictures in the book without their consent. Once again, if you see your picture and you are mad, please forgive me. Those people are all important to me, and my readers will know what they have done in private in my life. I pay tribute to many of them who have passed away.

The school and all its obligations, which were considered my responsibility according to my father, was hard to manage. Spending most of my evenings playing soccer, which is called football outside the USA; working in the farms during the rainy season; doing small businesses in the evenings; and so forth had occupied all my time for serious studies. Civil wars had caused class interruptions. During these class interruptions, an opportunity presented itself, and it was a source of income in the future. Missionary Claude Petman was responsible for providing food to the needy, especially the sick in the hospital. My brother-in-law's younger brother Jean and cousin Jess asked me to help them make food packaging for Claude Petman. This would become my first job. These activities did not last because we were replaced by Mr. Adinan in case the school resumed. As Claude Petman always needed help with small jobs, I continued to help him during my spare time. I considered this work to be a simple volunteering, especially since Mr. Claude set aside my salary without giving me, but I did not know. One day, he advised me to register at College Charles Lwanga (CCL), which was a private institution. It was a good idea to better invest my savings that he had, and it allowed me to study without interruptions of blank years and teachers' strikes. I had refused, but rather, I told him that in case I used all my savings and my father would be unable to sponsor me, they would kick me out. I had to buy a bike, so if he left the country, I would trade in the weekly markets of the surrounding villages. My ideas were appreciable, but he begged me to try the process anyway. Unfortunately, it did not go well. So finally, I bought the bike. Wanting to be wise in my own eyes, I suffered the consequences. A looting of the military had occurred at our house a year later, and they took my bike with the other stuff. The Bible says in Proverbs 3:5–7, "Trust in the Lord with all your heart and lean not on your own understanding. In all your ways acknowledge Him, and He shall direct your paths. Do not be wise in your own eyes; Fear the Lord and depart from evil" (NKJV). This apology confirmed what Dr. Myles Munroe said in *Understanding Your Place in God's Kingdom* (page 25), "Failure to establish correct priority causes you to waste your two most important commodities: your time and your energy. When your priorities are not correct, you will find yourself busy with the wrong things, majoring on the minor, doing unnecessary, or becoming preoccupied with the unimportant."

Having started school at the age six and the primary level was supposed to be done by age twelve, I had instead finished it at age fifteen. The high school grade consisting of first and second cycles—I had finished it in ten years instead of seven years. You have no idea, but you will have to ask yourself what. He had just expressed finishing high school, which should mean having the baccalaureate. No, I meant to stop, and I will explain it. The second cycle in the French-language school system is high school in the English-language system. I was in a scientific program, opting to do biology. After failing the first baccalaureate exam, I reregistered for the second chance. During the school year, I had made a vow to God. If I succeeded in the baccalaureate, I would study Bible with the students at the Bible school for a year before going to the university in the capital of Chad (N'Djamena). The one who helped me with the schoolbooks was the priest Géli of College Charles Lwanga (CCL). These schoolbooks, combined with personal effort, resulted in partial success on my second attempt of the baccalaureate. I was saying partial because I had to do the oral exam to confirm my final admission. Unfortunately, the oral examination was not positive.

During my prayers, I said, "O God, as I failed my baccalaureate, my promise for Bible school would be forgotten." For quite some time, I did not have peace.

I had to ask the pastor Moise Alndibaye. I told him, "Pastor, this school year that had just ended, I had told God that if I passed the baccalaureate, I would devote a year to the Bible school, and after that, I would go to university. But, Pastor, as you knew, I failed my baccalaureate."

Without delay, the pastor quoted the verse in Ecclesiastes 5:4–5: "When you make a vow to God, do not delay paying it; for He has no pleasure in fools. Pay what you have vowed. Better not to vow than to vow and not to pay." He had not helped me; my guilt had increased. He offered me a scholarship that would allow me to live at school dormitory with the other students. I had refused the offer, but I had decided to take the Bible courses by being external. The refusal was motivated by the idea of trying the scientific baccalaureate for the third time as a free candidate at the end of the school year. I should have obeyed what Proverbs said in 3:5–6: "Trust in the Lord with all your heart and lean not on your own understanding; in all your ways acknowledge Him, and He shall direct your paths." Then I would have avoided a lot of confusion. The third attempt of baccalaureate was chaotic because of the Bible school and little motivation mixed with hidden discouragement. I had an excellent result in the Bible school exams. The committee of the teachers wrote this on my end-year results paper: "God speaks to you through these results. Think!" This time, I refused to meditate on these words because I could have put myself in an opposition from which I cannot return. The pastoral work was nonprofit; no one would answer amen. If I responded yes to the committee, I would be in the ministry in full time. None of them had forced me, they just said, "Think!"

Project to Embrace a Healthcare Career Leading to My First Adventure to Goundi

A revelation had come to me, and I made my mind to bring back the borrowed books to Father Géli; that at the same time, I would beg him to negotiate my enrollment in the school of nurses of Goundi run by the other Catholic priests. Father Géli accepted the idea. He said, to make my registration official, I had to send a handwritten request. I had written it and gave it to the priest at the college the same day. These steps were taken in early July 1988. Back home, I was caught up in the farm until early September. Having no phone our communication with the priest to follow-up my request was impossible. CCL, being a private college, the doors had reopened in September. I had decided one morning to visit Father Géli and inquire about my application.

Seeing me at the doorstep of his office, he exclaimed, "Welcome, I've been waiting for you for a few days! Good news! Goundi was waiting for you too."

Immediately, he wrote a letter, sealed it, and gave it to me. He advised me to travel to Goundi in early October because nursing classes would have started at that time. I returned that day very happy; I had informed my father the project of this adventure. My dad was proud of my decision despite some opposition from other people, but the paternal yes was my strong support. I sold my goat and my shea nuts early, and having met the minimum of conditions, the journey had become imminent. What is not done in the West is to arrive as a guest at someone's house (relative or friend, whatever) without notifying him beforehand. This was my excuse for the fact that my trip was in a hurry, and I had no phone. Along the way, a young travel companion also went to the nursing school in Goundi. As he understood that I was going for the same purpose, he asked me who would be my host. I told him the name of a brother in Christ Moise Toingué, whom I had only met during the youth camps in the past.

The strange thing after these past encounters was that there was no exchange until the next opportunity. The one I had a close relationship with was his older brother because he was once the leader of our youth at my local church. Shortly after our conversation, we arrived in Goundi. My traveler companion's host family lived not far from where I was supposed to be. When I arrived, my friend had gone out, and as his younger brother did not know me, I had to introduce myself to him. He was not surprised because they were used to the improvisers who arrived home without telling them. I asked him to accompany me to the priest Ghérardi Angelo (the founder of the hospital in Goundi) while telling him the reason for my emergency. I wanted to hand over the sealed letter that the priest of CCL had given me. Upon our arrival, Father Ghérardi was somewhere in his business. His cook told us he would be coming home soon. The place was not far from my host, so I had decided to wait, and I let the little one go home. Half an hour later, Father Ghérardi was back. He was asking me the question at the door: Who did I want to see? I told him that I had this letter from Father Géli of Sarh's CCL. He said it was for him.

I would say, "Oh, fine."

He had read it, then he asked me where I would be staying. I told him the name of Moses. He added very well, as it was Saturday; he had given me a stapled note to give on Monday morning to the manager of the hospital, Andjibaye. Returning to my friend's concession, I was well fed and got a place to sleep. On Sunday morning, I went to worship at the Baptist Church where Moses, his sisters, and his brothers attended. My host was still single. On Monday morning, as my appointment with the manager was at nine o'clock, I was already in front of the office at eight in the morning. As people walked all over the hospital, I was considered a sick person. At eight thirty, someone in the office asked me if I was looking for a place or somebody. I said I was there for Manager Andjibaye. The person had taken me to the back office to meet him. After greeting him, I handed him the note. He had read it and told me that the father was asking him to talk to me about their hospital system before leaving me with Dr. Joseph to take care of me. The information given to me and the tour to do had lasted only an hour. Wanting to put me in contact with the doctor, the manager realized he was in the operating room. The manager thought it was best for me to stay close to the operating room and wait because we did not know what other circumstance would come after. The doctor would go out an hour later; the manager would hurry up and tell him everything about me. He wanted to go home for something, so I went with him to his home, which was close to the hospital. He had inquired about me and told me frankly that school would not start until his colleague Dr. Charles returned from his specialty training. He said he had good news for me. I would start helping them in the operating room, and at the same, I would be trained in radiology to replace the former nurse who would be assigned as head of the laboratory.

On Tuesday, I began my orientation to the operating room. Nurses Bolngar Malloum and Djotoingué Theophile trained me in their routine. My first week was observing and cleaning after each procedure. In two weeks, I was already involved in several actions. I was called at the same time as the whole team to work at late hours either at night or during the day. For the sake of information, my friends in OR told me that they doubted very much if, with my training in radiology, I could fulfill the goal set by the doctor. The mutation program was planned for a long time, but no one was able to master radiology. The nurse willingly refused to properly train the first candidates. Luckily for me, I was related to that nurse. Before I left for Goundi, my paternal uncle told me that I had their cousin there; as I did not know him, I had instead chosen my old friend's home to stay. A couple of weeks before my training, I had already talked with him while conveying greetings from home. My schedule with him had been done. Two months of training passed, and I had officially taken over radiology while continuing to help in OR. The joy of embracing the profession of my dream and earning a minimum wage monthly meant that a year had passed without realizing it.

My curiosity led me to ask if the academic year 1989–1990 courses would begin. There was no clear response from any of the officials. I observed a small change; I saw some new hires. They let me know that they were coming to school. The first quarter passed without hope. Another academic year was passing. Embracing this second year, I was a little tired to share my friend's house, which was always full by the people in his family and other strangers who came for their care. So I had claimed my accommodation. Without hesitation, the manager had offered me the two-bedroom house with the condition of welcoming another student when classes would begin. Indeed, one of the students in the class that followed ours a year later had occupied the other room. Right after my move, it was my turn to find myself in the same situation as my friend. Whenever there was an outpouring of guests at home, he asked me to accept a few. Finally, not only his guests but mine, especially those of my own family, flocked. Welcoming people was part of our life in Goundi.

In addition to working full time, I was also helping at the Pentecostal Church, which opened not too long before I arrived in October 1988. Keeping the same departments (surgery and radiology) for almost two years, the time had come for a change. A newly hired student had joined me to be trained in radiology and to work in OR. I had trained him well in record time and just before our real academic year 1990–1991. I was assigned to another department. I was worried and anxious about the occupations of the past two years, the church, the guests, and at the same time, the school that was to begin. But as Romans 8:28 says, "And we know that all things work together for good to those who love God." The other departments, such as pediatrics, medicine, dispensary, and maternity, where students had to take the internship for three to six months in turn did not require the extraordinary hours. However, I had enough time to study. With God's help, the repetitions of the senior year in the scientific school, the first two years of experience, and the seriousness put into the studies had helped me to be first in my class. My monthly salaries were below 10,000 francs CFA, which meant below

$20. In this first academic year, the students were informed that their monthly salaries as a scholarship were going to be 10,000 francs CFA ($20), the second year was 10,500 francs CFA ($21), and the third year was 11,000 francs CFA ($22). This was normal during training, but what was surprising was even the senior nurses hardly earned 15,000 francs CFA ($30) or 20,000 francs CFA ($40) per month. No one had paid for the training, and no word was heard about a refund. For the first time in the 1991–1992 class, the founder changed his mind. The school received government accreditation, and the priest knew that if he did not do something, all the laureates would leave the hospital after six months or a year for better pay working for the government. The condition of admission from this academic year was to work for the hospital five years after graduating. Those who would violate this law should reimburse the training before they would leave. I did not think it was especially relevant to me after working three years before the decision. You will understand later why I am mentioning this now.

As I mentioned my brilliant end to the first year, it had given me reassurance to finish the remaining two years well. I was beginning to think about choosing a friend who would become my wife. During my vacation with my parents at the end of class of the year 1991, I had decided to talk to the girl whose thought of proposing her did not leave my mind. The night before my second day, I prayed to God for a sign as Gedeon had done. In Judges 6:36–38, it says, "Gedeon said to God: If you want to deliver Israel by my hand, as you said, behold, I will put a fleece of wool in the area; if the fleece alone is covered with dew and all the land remains dry, I will know that you will deliver Israel by my hand as you said. And so, it came. The next day he got up early in the morning, pressed the fleece, and brought out the dew, which gave full water a cup." There had been two signs of Gedeon, but I had chosen this first one. For my case, I told God that if before the end of that day, Florence passed by my father's compound when she returned from the market, I would approach her to request my friendship with her. Early in the morning, I had knocked on my father's door, and he said come in. He knew I wanted to tell him something.

I immediately said to him, "Dad, I would like to court a girl you know well. I hadn't spoken to the girl yet, but I would do so when I had the opportunity."

He asked me the name of the girl, and I told him Florence Ngonbian (Ngonbian was the popular nickname of Florence's father who was my father-in-law).

After a silence, he said that I still had two years of schooling, and choosing a girl who had passed the puberty age, I would find myself after a few years with a woman apparently older than me. According to the custom, it is the man who should be older than the woman. It does not matter the difference (four to fifteen or twenty years) but not the opposite. To convince him, I told him that I would try, and if possible, we would be together before the so-called wilting of the girl. Our conversation ended behind closed doors, and no one else in the family asked me about my intention because neither Dad nor I mentioned it. I had bathed and dressed as I was going to go out for a visit. Near noon, the impatience was going to win me, but I had tried to wait a little longer. Suddenly, I saw Florence entering our compound. She greeted us and said that someone had told her that I had come. As she was in a hurry, I accompanied her with the idea of telling her what I planned to do that day. I told her I wanted to be her friend. She said there was no problem. I also added that once I left for Goundi, I would start sending her correspondences. As my stays were extended with my friends, we made a visit to her family, and it was an opportunity to see her once again before my return trip. The first weekend, as I had friends who used to go to the weekly market, I gave my first letter to a friend for Florence, and this means of communication was the only one for us because neither she nor I had a telephone (home or mobile).

The courses of the 1991–1992 academic year resumed, and my practice continued in new departments. My results were always good but in second position. As there was Florence who had added to my travel priorities, I had still gone on vacation at the end of classes in 1992 to physically strengthen the relationship. Practically, one year had passed. Normally, my parents had to ask for her hand to fulfill my commitment to her, but nothing had happened, which was not normal according to the custom. Being away from Florence, I did not know that other suitors wanted to do coup d'état, a way of saying that they were also dating her to win my girl of choice. The last academic year, 1992–1993, was a year of important decisions. I had finished the first semester well, but in the second semester, Florence and her niece Florence Bidaina had come for the Easter break, but they were staying with the cousin Zara, Dr. Rimtebaye's wife. It was on this occasion that I asked my friend if she wanted to be my fiancée. Do not ask me what the sign of that commitment was. To tell the truth, it was verbal because I did not have an engagement ring. Nothing else had happened between us, as was customary for all young people. Her yes bounced the ball to my side. My parents and I should customarily materialize by sending the first part of dowries and the hand request. What she had not told me was reported by my friend who visited her during his trip to Sarh because they had already met in Goundi during Easter. She confessed that I chose her but without realizing anything toward her parents, so she did not know if I was serious about my choice. The friend, on his return, brought me the news in full. We immediately joined forces with my parents to send the partial dowries to his family. The completion of the dowries took place later.

The people who are not familiar with the term *dowry* might need this explanation. In the village, most of the time, the girls are surprised by men sometimes without exchanges of speech beforehand.

One morning, the girl could be called by the parents who would say to her, "Such a man sent this delegation asking for your hand. What would your answer be?"

The girl could say yes or no, and the delegation would return with or without what they brought or the stuff would follow them if the girl wanted time to think and would say no afterward.

All this is to explain that neither a negative response nor my money was returned. Our exchange of letters continued, but unfortunately, my trusted friend stopped trading in Goundi, so I chose another local boy who was an apprentice. He wanted to turn away my fiancée for himself. I later understood that many letters were lost without fair explanations.

I mentioned that this was the year of important decisions; the second one was to welcome my niece and my little brother. One of my cousins came from the village to get medical care in Goundi, accompanied by his wife and two of his children, which meant he had several others left in the village. The doctor informed me that his diagnosis was cancer and that he had less than six months to live. The doctor treated him for about two months and discharged him. I held a family council with them and suggested that they would leave the girl with me as she was old enough to cook food. My hidden goal was to keep one of the children in case my cousin died. It is natural even now in Africa that when a husband dies, generous family members decide to share children who are not very small and in need of protection and education. My niece Allaren stayed, and it was advantageous because I had enough time to study instead of thinking about cooking food myself as I did before. The second member of my family would be my younger brother who would come later.

The third decision was due to the reminder of the appreciation made by the administration at the end of Bible school mentioned in the first chapters of the book about my life in high school. This appreciation said, "God speaks to you through these results. Think about it!" It was getting strong in me so much that I meditated on going to Bible school again. This time, I was thinking about the one in N'Djamena, the capital of Chad, named Bible School Esdras of N'Djamena (BSEN) and led by the missionary Ribaye. Having mentioned the idea to my local pastor, Director Ribaye was already aware, and he hoped to welcome me in October 1993. There was a mixture of human wisdom. The results of my first two semesters of the third year of nursing school put me in second place, so I thought it would be that rank that I would occupy until the final. I prayed to God. If I would be first in my class, I would go to the BSEN; otherwise, I would not go. Keeping the same determination in studies, God in his Sovereignty made me come out first in the academic year-end exams. After the graduation ceremony, I tried to explain my situation to Father Gherardi, the founder of the hospital, thinking he would appreciate the idea; unfortunately, he had categorically opposed. He even increased my burden. He said that if I would persist in leaving, I would have to pay a million francs CFA, which was $2,000, if not, prison. I let him know that my goal was a leave of absence for one academic year (from October 1993 to June 1994) and come back to live the rest of my life serving God and work in the hospital forever. He did not understand, so I finally felt it was pointless to insist. As a graduated, Father Ghérardi imposed a monthly payment on the house I used to occupy for free. I had to rent a house with metal roof and two houses in straws elsewhere to live with my niece and my younger brother.

As the Bible school project failed, I wanted to speed things up and get married. I knew that financially, I was not ready, but the idea was that since my future wife had the senior year high school level, she could enroll in the same nursing school, and our two salaries could help us support our household. I had taken a credit, and with my savings, it was going to be enough for a modest Christian wedding ceremony. My fiancée was informed of my plan. I had rushed to send to people my invitation tickets three months before September 1993, which was the likely month of the ceremony. The communication, which was only by mail, created a misunderstanding that thwarted everything that was planned. Florence sent a letter explaining her preparation plan, but I had not received her letter.

At my shift from 6:00 a.m. to 6:00 p.m., my colleague, who was also related to Florence and had heard me brag about my future wedding, said to me, "Nouba I'm sorry to inform you, but your brothers- and sisters-in-law said that your fiancée had to go on to school to have her high school diploma. What wedding at that time to a man in a village of Goundi?"

Once I heard those words, I became mentally ill. I was no longer in control, seeing that I was gradually becoming a danger to the sick to the point of making medical errors. I asked permission to go and talk to my doctor, who was an Italian. I explained my situation to him and asked him for permission to travel immediately to Sarh to hear from my fiancée what her family members said.

The doctor said, "Nouba, leave tonight, go, and resolve this situation."

I had come back to apologize to my colleagues and to my charge nurse. They understood me well and wished me a safe trip. For any trip before Sunday (day of market) from Goundi to Sarh, any passenger is obliged to travel to Koumra and take another transportation to continue. The headquarters of our Pentecostal Church was in this town of Koumra. As I learned that a conference would have taken place there, I had an insight of not to stay with the parents of my host Moses of Goundi but to spend my night in church, where I could see friends who would have come to the meeting. I was already at Koumra before 6:00 p.m. My older sister's former friend who lived near the church had offered me water to bathe. It would be difficult for some to understand, but in Chad, for most people, you take water in a bucket, and to take a shower, there is no shower room like in Western countries.

After my bath, I should eat. Before I moved close to the dining table, a group of young women came from a village called Bedaya. As I knew them, they were amazed to see me again. I asked them if it was only their group that traveled; one of them who knew nothing about my relationship with Florence said that there was one of her comrades from Sarh with her younger brother in the truck, but they were passing for Moundou.

When I heard to Moundou, it stunned me because one of my fiancée's big brothers lived in Moundou. I asked for the name, and she told me it was Florence. As I knew that drivers would stop at every major station during their trip, I was convinced to find them before they continued. Walking fast, I had arrived at the parking lot, and there they sat on the bench. I greeted them, and she was surprised to see me.

She asked me where I came from, I said, "From Goundi, and just for you."

I told her that I had questions for her and asked if we could talk in private. We had strayed but not very far so we could watch the other passengers in case they would take off.

I had gone straight to my pertinent question: "Florence, are you still my fiancée?"

"Why not?" she replied. She added, "What was this kind of question?"

I took a big breath, and I told her that I was at work in the morning, and we were chatting with my colleague Isabelle, her relative. As I mentioned to her the plan for our marriage, she told me that she was sorry to tell me that your brothers and sisters said that you had to continue your studies to get your baccalaureate. "What wedding in a village of Goundi?" they added.

Very surprised and shocked by speculation, Florence replied, "These were all lies. As you had set the date of our marriage, I had advocated traveling to Goundi to tell you about my plans. Unfortunately, your cousin Pastor Enoch prevented me from traveling. I sent you a long letter to explain that I would go to Moundou to my big brother's house to collect gifts that he prepared for my wedding."

I replied that I had not received the so-called letter. The letter was given to the young man who wanted to outwit Florence on his own account or on the account of his boss driver. I did not know. What a change in atmosphere at that moment. As their truck was ready to continue the journey, I gave her a goodbye kiss, and I was relieved and went back to my resting place. Who would imagine this miracle of our meeting in Koumra? Suggesting that we had not seen each other and that I arrived in Sarh at her absence, in addition to not receiving convincing explanations, especially since the phone calls were not available neither to me nor to her. Besides, her brother from Moundou did not know me at the time, and I did not know his phone number to call. God coordinated everything for his glory. In the morning, from Koumra, I continued to Sarh to visit my parents as my urgent leave of absence was for one week. After my short stay, I went back to Goundi. No kidding, there was no more communication between Florence and me because the means by letter was impossible. After a month, I thought maybe the speculations were true and that my fiancée herself did not know.

Suddenly, the Bible studies project at BSEN came back to my mind strongly. I requested a leave of absence (LOA) for a month. I was granted the LOA, as this time, my younger brother went back to my parents in Sarh, and it was only my niece who stayed with me. I informed my pastor, my close friends, and my niece that my goal was to go to N'Djamena. When I got there, I would speak frankly to the director of BSEN about the threat of legal action by Father Ghérardi. If the director got scared and did not welcome me, I would take the opportunity to visit my older sister and her family and return to Goundi again after I had finished my LOA. In case he kept me, I would take the courses for an academic year before returning. I reassured my niece that if I stayed, I would arrange for her to join my parents in Sarh. Oddly enough, my niece had to stay alone in my place but under the care of the family of my friend who resigned one year ago. Having arranged everything, I left Goundi; some members of the administration knew this, but as I was hesitant about the response of the Director of N'Djamena, I told them to keep it secret until it would be confirmed first, and then they could inform Father Ghérardi. I traveled to Sarh to my parents and informed them of my travel goal in N'Djamena. After resting for two days, I set off for N'Djamena. Throughout my life, it was my second trip to the capital after the one I made in 1984 during the Christian youth camp.

NEXT ADVENTURE IN THE CAPITAL N'DJAMENA

I am talking about October 1994. I cannot remember the day I arrived, but it was an afternoon that we had arrived at the bus station. I took a taxi to Main Apostolic Church, where the Bible school was located, and it was also there that the missionary director of BSEN was staying with his family. God being good, He made a brother in Christ, Adoumkidjim, former colleague from the high school Ahmed Mangué. He was there before me. After a warm welcome, I asked him to introduce me to the director since I had never met before.

As we were walking toward the house to meet the missionary, I took the opportunity to ask him for his program, with the intention that he accompany me to my older sister's house, and he was very happy to give me ride. To the principal, I introduced myself as a student from Goundi. Immediately, I told him there was a condition. It was to refer to my situation to be liable to the legal proceedings of Father Ghérardi when I applied for a leave of absence. The director said that my pastor in Goundi had told him about my coming since last year (1993), and that the year passed without seeing me.

If this year (1994) I could arrive, he would not let me go again. He told me I should not be afraid. After this reassurance, I was sure of my admission. I paid the required tuition, and immediately, my friend accompanied me to my sister who was not even aware of my arrival in N'Djamena. The moment she saw me, she was happy and amazed. I explained to her everything and that I came to the Bible school, which meant that I was not their direct guest. My friend took me back to the BSEN before going home. The principal introduced me to the internal students and their leader. After the evening meal, we were directed to our dormitory, which was in another neighborhood. The day after I arrived, more than a dozen other students joined us (the four internal students) in class. Both external and internal students were entitled to lunch, except for the internal ones, who had breakfast and dinner as well. My stays seemed guaranteed because my training, my accommodation, and my food were sponsored almost entirely by the school because the 12,000 francs CFA ($24) was nothing compared to all expenses. I had been involved in my studies. As in many of our Pentecostal congregations, there were Saras (major tribe of Southern Chad). I had become one of the interpreters everywhere we went as a group of students. Another activity was evangelism.

As the training was scheduled for three quarters, we found ourselves already at the end of the first trimester. Behind me, a friendship had been made between Father Ghérardi and my cousin Pastor Enoch. To my surprise, the father stepped up his threats through my cousin. He instructed him to write a long letter whose central point was to make me leave the Bible school immediately; otherwise, I had to pay 1,000,000 francs CFA ($2,000) or I would go to jail. After reading all the content, I left the group and entered the chapel, which was vacant at the time. I had knelt to pray. About thirty minutes, I got up to present the letter to the director.

He read it, and calmly, he said to me, "Don't worry, Nouba." For a few weeks after this intimidation by the letter, I thought that one day the police would come and take me to lock me up because my decision was to continue my Bible school. Neither another threatening letter nor the lawmen have disturbed me yet.

It was already the second trimester, and my plan was to take advantage of the Easter break to go directly to Goundi to apologize and beg Father Ghérardi to let me work at the end of the training. In the midterm, our school welcomed a guest speaker from Koumra, Pastor

Levi Manitha. His first day was the contact, his personal testimony, and an introduction to his topic. We came home that evening to rest. In the middle of the night, I had a dream. The dream told me I was going to die. I woke up and prayed. Shortly before the rooster singing, the same dream was repeated. The voice said, "You will die, and it is because you are a servant of God that you are warned." I was scared and prayed until the morning.

After breakfast, we went to class. The message began following a period of praise and worship. Instead of continuing the topic, the guest speaker changed the subject by talking about how to act during attacks. As he also lived in Europe, he said that someone had entered a compound during a door-to-door evangelization. The man saw a very threatening dog ready to pounce on him. He kept saying as he walked toward the dog, "I bind you in the name of Jesus." The dog stopped barking and lied down quietly. These examples of attack continued until the break period.

When all my friends had gone out for break, I went to him and said that the Lord had guided him to strengthen me. I told him that I had twice the same dream with the warning that I would die. The second time I heard that, it was because I am a servant of God that he warned me. He immediately began to take authority over my life, and I knelt while praying too. The friends curiously asked me what was going on, and I explained it to them.

The second term was over, and luckily, the school provided the transportation money. As planned, I decided to travel with the other students in a large truck that carried the goods. This meant that we passengers were in the open air above these goods (natron and salt) and luggage. We had started late at night, so we had to spend the night on the way. In the morning, we continued the journey that was to last because of the long distance that remained to be covered. Another stop allowed some to relieve themselves in the toilet and others, like Muslims, to pray. No one knew what the driver did during the pose, whether he was on drugs or getting drunk. Before boarding the cabin, he would tell Muslim passengers that their next prayer would be made at the destination (City of Sarh). His plan was to drive at full speed, but no one knew. As he was in his cabin separated from all, he began to risk our lives. The speed of the truck suddenly interrupted the noisy chat of all passengers of about forty people. After a straight stretch of road, we reached a curve very abruptly. Maybe it was fear or whatever hit me, but I stood up from my spot, and I could see the truck meandering. I knew something was wrong.

Suddenly, I started shouting very loudly, "Jesus, Jesus, Jesus!"

A woman close to me was also shouting the name of Jesus. A burst of noise was heard, and it was the truck that overturned its wheels in the air away from the road about forty-five feet in the bush. The place was filled with dust. I did not know where we were, finding myself kneeling at a six-foot distance from the truck. The dust dissipated, and when I raised my head, I could see people bathed in blood screaming from everywhere. Some bodies did not move. One of them was the husband of the woman who was praying at the same time as me. I could see one of my fellow students, but I did not see the second one as there were three of us among the passengers. I was beginning to call his name, "Jeremie, Jeremie!"

I saw a good part of his body under the body of the truck, and his head was outside. I called for help, we tried to pull him out, but we could not because he was stuck. The ground was hard, so we softened by digging under him. Finally, with some effort, we were able to pull him out and bring him to the shade of the tree. I spoke to his ear, urging him to say, "Jesus, save me." I had him repeat this several times. The police was alerted, thanks to the other drivers passing by. A rescue vehicle had arrived. All the injured were embarked, then the uninjured, and finally, the nine dead people, including the driver and his apprentice. My colleague unfortunately became the tenth person to die after surgery the same night at Sarh Hospital. Once again, it was an unannounced trip to my parents, to whom I had just come to visit before continuing to Goundi as planned. Once I got home that night, my parents, not knowing anything about what happened, were happy to see me. As I sat down, I burst into tears. I was screaming loudly that my mom did not know what was going on. She absolutely wanted to understand what happened to me.

My dad tried to tell her, "Let him cry. He'll tell us once he calms down." Almost an hour and thirty minutes later, I washed my face, and I told them everything from my past two and a half months ago and the confirmation of the warning dream. I told them that they had just missed an unexpected grief and sadness. The other cause of my crying was the condition of my colleague who ended very badly, leaving behind him his wife and children. To reassure myself, I had gone to the hospital where I was given some anti-inflammatory drugs to relieve the pain I was beginning to feel in my legs and feet. It was a shock to Florence, as she had already returned from Moundou. She was imagining that she was going to lose a fiancé like that. I took the opportunity to explain this change of decision and at the same time apologize for taking it without informing her. I did not stay long in Sarh, and I continued after a few days in Goundi to settle my situation after the Bible school training. Once I arrived in the evening, I asked for an audience to see Father Ghérardi. He welcomed me in his office, and I began to apologize for my disobedient attitude to his orders. I asked him to excuse me and allow me to come back in June 1994 to resume my work.

In anger, he said, "I will never take you back, and before you leave Goundi, you will pay my 1,000,000 CFA francs [$2,000]."

I also raised my voice by saying, "By tomorrow I will leave, and I will not pay anything because the order to pay for the training was not in my contract. It was a decision made after my batch."

I had hurried to go out as I had become an enemy instead of being the returning prodigal child quoted in Luke 15:18–22, I will arise and go to my father, and will say to him, 'Father, I have sinned against you against heaven and before you, and I am no longer worthy to be called your son. Make me like one of your hired servants.' And he arose and came to his father. But when he was still a great way off, his father saw him and had compassion and ran and fell on his neck and kissed him. And the son said to him, 'father, I have sinned against heaven and your sight, and am no longer worthy to be called your son. But the father said to his servants, bring out the best robe and put it on him, and put a ring on his hand and sandals on his feet. And bring the fatted calf here and kill it and let us eat and be merry. For this my son was dead and he is alive again; he was lost and is found; and began to be merry.

A terrible depression won me because I knew the influence of this priest in Goundi. He could tell the gendarmerie brigade to lock me up if I kept traveling without signing the refund liability. The next morning, I did not rush to the travel agency thinking that the suggestion of the night was going to be fulfilled. Another white friend of Father Ghérardi, who lived in the surroundings, had his wife ill; unfortunately, she died the same night. The priests' compound was agitated in the morning, and the news came to us that there was a case of death in their circle. I quietly arranged my belongings and went to the travel agency to take my departure back to Sarh. Arriving in Sarh, I did not delay, and I traveled to N'Djamena for the rest of my courses. Knowing that my return to Goundi after the Bible training would be impossible, I decided to activate the idea I had about my professional practice. My Thursdays being free, I negotiated to volunteer at the general hospital. My integration was finally possible through a relative, Doctor Odile.

During Bible school, I only went on Thursdays until we finished the academic year in June 1995. At the end of the course, the director of BSEN gave us money for our travel back to our provinces. Having my conflict with Goundi, I could not go back. So I told the director that I was going to stay a little longer in N'Djamena with my sister Ruth Baroumbaye and her husband, Badé Toningar, who were both sick. Instead of joining them, I decided to rent the house of one of our classmates. I was beginning to assume my responsibilities, so I must use wisdom. I asked for a job at the orphanage, which was to clean the rooms, and assumed the role of night watchman. I continued to volunteer at the hospital as well. The idea of renting the house away from my relatives was not accepted by them because my little sister Pulcherie would have to cross a long distance every day to bring me the meal because I was no longer in charge of the Bible school. My brother-in-law rented me a house close to their compound.

In terms of church activities, I joined the women's group. "Mary has chosen the right part." I attended their meeting every Wednesday. Finally, I made myself useful in N'Djamena. Other thoughts had come to me. I suggested to the apostle Leon responsible of N'Djamena region that I wanted to open a prayer cell in the courtyard of my brother-in-law as an access to worship. The idea was appreciated, and we started to meet on Tuesdays.

Strikes by civil servants took place in July 1995, and this affected health institutions as well. One Thursday, I was with the other nurses, and one of their colleagues was coming in. His acquaintances welcomed him happily. They asked him about his place of work at the Order of Malta Amtoukoui (private health institution). He told the others about the death of one of their nurses, which meant that they had closed their doors because of the circumstance. I waited until the visiting nurse Masrayam was finished and was about to leave. I followed him to the door and told him that I was interested in working in Amtoukoui, so I would like to ask for his help for my integration. His answer was not satisfactory. He told me that they had a very hard religious leader and that where I was should be better for me. I did not insist, and I let him go. Next Thursday following my meeting with this nurse from Amtoukoui, I went back to the hospital continuously for my volunteering. The charge nurse gave me instructions to execute. He had not yet moved away that I saw a white religious sister intercepting him. I listened to these words: "I'm looking for a nurse from Koumra who works here."

The charge nurse replied, "We have no one from Koumra in our group, but the young man you see there"—pointing his finger at me—"came from Goundi."

The sister added, "Can I talk to him?" The charge nurse said, "Yes, go ahead."

Without delay, the visitor entered. She introduced herself, saying her name was Sister Helen, and asked me, "Do you want to work with me in Amtoukoui?"

Without hesitation, I said yes, and immediately, I remembered my conversation with the nurse who visited our hospital last week. Very happy with my answer, she recommended that I bring my handwritten application and my diploma to the Embassy Order of Malte, then I had to localize the Health Center of Amtoukoui and go there on the Monday following the day of our meeting at 9:00 a.m. at the center. She took me to her driver who explained to me how to find the embassy. Like somewhere in my writing, I said that addresses in Chad were difficult to find. You had to follow the plan according to the key points of reference—banks, offices, number of roads to cross, and so forth. What excitement! I told the good news to the charge nurse and told him I should leave immediately. When I got to my house, I entered in my sister's room as she was sick, and I informed her of everything that had happened. Without delay, I found my diploma, wrote a handwritten application, went to the main market to make the photocopy, and put everything in the envelope. With the help of the taxi driver, I was able to find the embassy and submitted my job application the same day.

As scheduled, the following Monday, I was already at the health center before 9:00 a.m. I talked to a man in scrubs, and he put me around the corner to wait for the manager. A few minutes after 9:00 a.m., I saw the same sister heading inside. She asked question about me, and Gilbert, the man in scrubs, brought me in directly. I immediately recognized the nurse I had met ten days ago, and immediately, I thanked him because I knew that it was through him that I found this job despite his negative response on the first day. As there were two nurses (one with the children and the other with the adults), the sister recommended that they took turns observing how I handled shots and wound dressings. Their observation lasted only about two hours, and they were satisfied with my practice. The first day had already gone well, and I came back home happy. As I started in the middle of August at the end of this month, the sister handed me an envelope of 17,000 francs CFA ($34). Half of my first salary even exceeded the monthly salaries I was earning being in Goundi. The following months, my salary was increased to 35,000 francs CFA ($70) until the end of 1995.

On the spiritual side, I continued to lead the prayer cell and to assist the women in their weekly activities. During my absence from the south of the country, my fiancée lost her father; finally, she decided to join her brothers in N'Djamena to continue her studies. Having become an employee, the idea of getting married became stronger and stronger in me. When the financial resources increased, the needs also increased. I already had the bicycle's loan. The small room I occupied had to be replaced by a house of at least two bedrooms, as I was considering a future wedding. My first half of 1996, I struggled to add the dowry but not in full, and since my fiancée was close to me, time allowed us to agree on many things before our union and our life as a couple. In the way that each young person was fighting, my fiancée who did not want to be only a housewife had tried the test of teaching program for the field of elementary education. For the wedding ceremony, I could not count on my savings, so I began to inform the acquaintances, the spiritual leaders, especially the women's group, and my workplace. Noticing the huge manner of the wedding ceremonies in N'Djamena, I had a panic attack, and I instead suggested to my apostle Leon to bless us at the church, imitating my best friend who carried out his wedding not very long in this way before signing the papers at the commune (town hall) later. The date of the ceremony was scheduled for Saturday, October 12, 1996. In the month of September and at the beginning of October, a lot of contributions came in, and at the same time, the different groups did their rehearsals, and the culinary group prepared everything. A former friend should be my bridegroom, and my fiancée also chose her former friend as the bride's friend.

The private sector paid well but not to take time off from work as you wish. I was obliged to ask my cousin to prepare the wedding costumes. The missionary Remy and the in-law's family had arranged their vehicles free of charge for our transport after the wedding. Having only one motorbike, my friend delayed because he wanted to take his family to the Apostolic Church of Moursal, the place of the wedding, before coming to pick me up. He was late, and my fiancée was already waiting for me outside the door at the time indicated for the ceremony. I was told later that people were wondering if I had changed my mind about our marriage. All were astonished that it was the fiancée who was waiting for the fiancé. When we appeared, I remained like a dry wood in motion. A moment that must have been joyful for me was as if I was accompanying a dead person to the cemetery. My first smile only appeared when we were asked to make our vows. The preacher asked me the question, and I answered, "Yes, yes."

While it was my fiancée's turn, she did not raise her voice by saying yes. That was when the interpreter in Sara made a small comment that excited the room to burst out laughing. This moment became a relief for me until the end of the ceremony. When we were done inside, people ate finger food in the churchyard. Before it was very dark because of the lack of electricity, the vehicles took us home. The next day, another great party took place as is customary. All that was done according to tradition was already marriage, but the marriage certificate, not being signed, this should not be considered legal. We did not worry at that time, but at another opportunity, we would do it to be legal.

None of you expected to hear what was going to happen less than fifteen days after our wedding ceremony. My wife was coming home one evening more or less excited. She waited until our bedtime to inform me of the news. She said that she passed teaching program test that she did before our union. The bad news was that she had to be trained in Moundou (another big city very far from N'Djamena, the capital). Knowing the realities of Chad, no reasonable Chadian could let go of such an opportunity. We kept the hope that the older brothers could succeed to convince the authorities of this department to allow her to be trained in N'Djamena. The deadline was coming to an end without hope. My spiritual collaborators, especially the missionary of Switzerland, told me that he would never let his wife go away from him after less than a month of marriage. Knowing that the realities were different, I let my wife go at the beginning of November, and I was again alone but not like a single. The financial aid was used to pay for her transportation and my food. Her niece Amina Bidaina, being in Moundou, was the one who welcomed her. We were able to celebrate Christmas and the 1997 New Year together. She returned for the Easter break (March) to be the bride's friend. This bride was her former friend from school, but they are also related. The stays were initially short, with lots of other programs, but it was very enjoyable for us as a couple. The absence of both of us from each other had set fire to our marital duties.

Without thinking about her current studies, she left pregnant. Pregnancy revealed a few months after her return. As a husband, I helped financially as much as I could. She, benefiting from a government grant, managed to get by with the help of her niece. I could not even ask for permission to visit because of my working condition and insufficient financial resources. You will be surprised, but even at the birth of our first daughter, Sephora, on December 8, 1997, I saw only her photo.

I only had the chance to talk with my wife using the home phone of a minister cousin, Mr. Mirangaye Nadjalta. Florence understood my situation. Violating the condition of our private medical center was risking a dismissal. The travel money could help to buy necessities for the baby. Knowing this reality, she did not get angry. It was difficult for all of us, but we must deal with it.

I am going to talk a little bit about the choice of name. During our Bible reading, we read the story of Sephora, the wife of Moses, in Exodus 18:2–3: "Then Jethro, Moses' father-in-law, took Zipporah, Moses' wife, after he had sent her back, with her two sons, of whom the name of one was Gershom (for he said, 'I have been a stranger in a foreign land')." We had said that if God gave us a daughter, we would name her Sephora. Let us go back to our line of thought.

Christmas 1997 and New Year 1998, as I said before, Florence and Sephora could not travel to N'Djamena, and neither could I go to Moundou. Anyway, for Easter break, they had come to spend a few days with me, and that was when I kissed my eldest daughter for the first time. It is sad to say it in this book, but it was a reality. You will be surprised to know later, but the same thing would happen during the delivery of the other two of my children caused by different circumstances. What demeaned my worries was my intense preoccupations at work and at church. Missionary Remy, who was the new director of BSEN, became interested in our prayer cell. He brought students once a week to evangelize or sometimes to preach. He kept telling me that a church would be opened in my Abena neighborhood and that I would be in charge. It was not my idea, but by encouraging me, I understood that God chose me for a work greater than the prayer cell. There was an empty space next to us. The Bible school and the existing churches in N'Djamena organized an evangelical crusade. The gained souls should gather somewhere. As the offerings and tithes of the prayer cell were considerable, we asked to rent the same empty land whose owner was one of our new converts. A straw shed was built.

On Sundays, we put in the benches for our meeting, and after the service, we kept them at my brother-in-law's house. It was a heavy burden, but the support of other mature Christians who joined us and became the elders and deacons had lightened the burden on me.

The difficulties of the rainy seasons forced us to rent a neighbor's house to continue our weekly meeting. The crusade brought in new members, and as the old Christians joined us as well, it had increased our number. The denomination of our churches, The Chadian Apostolic Churches, was not organized in such a way as to pay church leaders, so each local church organized itself in its own way. Our policy in our local assembly was to adopt the method of the apostle Paul. We have called our Church, Tent and Disciples-Maker. The idea was based on Acts 18:1–4: "After these things Paul departed from Athens and went to Corinth. And he found a certain Jew named Aquila, born in Pontus, who had recently come from Italy with his wife Priscilla (because Claudius had commanded all the Jews to depart from Rome);

and he came to them. So because he was of the same trade, he stayed with them and worked; for by occupation, they were tentmakers. And he reasoned in the synagogue every sabbath and persuaded both Jews and Greeks." Another passage is in Acts 20:33–35: "I have coveted no one's silver or gold or apparel. Yes, you yourselves know that these hands have provided for my necessities, and for those who were with me. I have shown you in every way, by laboring like this, that you must support the weak people. And remember the words of the Lord Jesus, that He said, 'It is more blessed to give than to receive.'"

The sin of stealing happened in my life. It was by faith that I decided not to depend on the Church. In the early days, at my workplace, being a new employee, I was strict in refusing bribes. I was only satisfied with my salary. When my wife and daughter had returned permanently between June and July 1998, they were accompanied by a nanny who had to take care of the baby in case Florence found a job. My coworkers continued to benefit not only from the bribe's money but from a few vials of medicines, and they always tempted me to take my share. Finally, I gave in, and I was taking my share. The devil told me I had become a father, and it is said in the Bible in 1 Corinthians 9:9: "For it is written in the law of Moses, 'You shall not muzzle an ox while it treads out grain.'" The same law of Moses says in Exodus 20:15, "You shall not steal." As I refused to listen to the voice of the Holy Spirit inwardly, he remained silent for a long time. God in his love convinced me at a certain time. I abstained for a while and then fell back into the same practices again. God loved me so much and convinced me to repent sincerely, and I was able to see his blessing hand in the years following my repentance.

Let us go back to my family life: In September 2000, we had our second son, Kelita, whose name was chosen in the same way as Sephora's. His name was chosen through Nehemiah 10:10: "Their brethren: Shebaniah, Hodijah, Kelita, Pelaiah, Hanan." His birth took place in N'Djamena, so it was in my presence. The year 2001 was a year of extraordinary blessings. Always remaining faithful to the service of

God, he put strongly in my heart to try not the scientific baccalaureate again but the literary baccalaureate, which is called in Chad, Bac A. The results were posted, and I finally passed the exam. The same year, my wife was chosen to participate in the AGLO Conference in the United States. Our small economies and the donations from that women's organization made possible the trip planned for September 2001. The flight was supposed to take place on September 11. Unfortunately, the events of 9/11 in New York blocked it.

A day later, they had still traveled with her comrade. They only attended the closing of the conference in Houston. A family from Chad welcomed them, so they spent a few days there after the conference. On their way back to the country, they stopped in Paris, France, and spent days with her friend's children. The absence lasted almost a month. As soon as they returned, the company Air France reimbursed them for the damages caused by the flight delay. Since I already had a bike from the beginning of my job, my wife used this money to buy hers. We also bought another empty lot because the one I built on a year after her return from professional school of Moundou was only half a lot. I mentioned the purchase of the lot because it has become an important asset in my journeys. As I worked a few years in the private health center, and I found out that I had missed a lot of opportunities (physical assistance to my own family, church conferences at our headquarters, remote funerals, and others). I applied for my integration into the state workforce. In the USA, it is like working as a federal employee. I did not get a result quickly, so I maintained my position the health center Amtoukoui.

Quickly, before I mention the coming of third child, another religious sister called Mathilde replaced Sister Helen, my previous boss. She was very attached to the staff. My wife and I did not wait three years for the birth spacing, which was why, in September 2002, our third child was born, and she was named Mathilde in memory of the generous religious sister. Every time a child was born, my wife hired nannies in addition to the children of our relatives who stayed with us because we sent them to school like our children. It was part of the culture—many people to feed with few resources, but God always intervened.

The divine intervention at the beginning of 2003 made my integration to the state workforce a reality. In the eyes of my readers, they will think that I have fallen into a kind of stealing again. This time, "stealing the government." As it was normal in Chad, my conscience remained calm. My point is that if the civil employees received the government's salary, I received mine even though I continued working at the same health center. The government's money was not guaranteed because the delays in the state's salary were repeated every year. Considering this government failure, my bosses continued to pay my salary for the service rendered. If there were no strikes some months of the year and the government paid us, I had the favor of earning two salaries to support my family. On the side of the church, the same missionary who helped during his stay in Chad to open the church, as he went back to Switzerland, our elder's college made a request for money to buy the church's land, and they responded positively. It was an independence because we stopped renting elsewhere for our meetings. In that same year of 2003, I was ordained with all the other leaders of our churches in N'Djamena as pastor of my local assembly.

ANOTHER WIND OF ADVENTURE BEGINS TO BLOW

This pastoral anointing will change my decisions in relation to work in 2004. Before what is going to be said happened, I attended a gathering to hear a report of the pastors' meeting at our headquarters in Koumra. Pastor Daniel Rimbarngaye who participated told us about the important points, one of which was the opportunity to do biblical studies in Cameroon. After this meeting, I proposed a very dynamic young person who I knew at the main Apostolic Church. The apostle Leon told me that we should pray for the guidance of God and the conviction of that young guy. After our conversation, I did not hear anything as an answer from him. As of June 26, 2004, I had just returned from a seminar organized by our church; I had finished eating and had gone to take a shower. I was still in the shower when I heard a soft voice: It would be you who would benefit from the scholarship to go to the Bible College in Cameroon. Another thought came to my mind, *You fast tomorrow, and at the end of the fasting, you will talk to the ministries.* From that moment, the spiritual struggle began in me, but several other ideas convinced me, and I ended up saying, "Let the will of God be done in the name of Jesus Christ."

Attending the Sunday service, the preacher spoke about Jeremiah at the potter's house. Here were his comments: Jeremiah was ordered to go to the potter. He did not object. He did not ask why God sent him. One must obey the word of God. Absence of anointing, absence of glory. In his words, he continued to say, "Refusing to take a step with God and wanting the blessing it does not work. God wants to prune our bumps and beautify us." Ecclesiastes 11:1 says, "Cast your bread upon the waters, for you will find it after many days." And Ecclesiastes 11:4 says, "He who observes the wind will not sow, and he who regards the clouds will not reap." When I met my two apostles separately, the first one told me that he was thinking of me when they received the news. The second said that he mentioned my name to the missionary, but he told him that I had just been integrated into the public service, so my choice was not at a good time. Understanding that I was voluntarily available, he was very happy. On the way back, I explained everything to my wife how the idea came to me. She did not say a word to me. I was worried but had not tried forcing to hear her answer.

Late at night, she woke me up and said, "Nouba, I do not agree with your decision. It's madness. You are now doing God's work, and isn't that enough for you? Have not you seen all these servants suffering? If you insist on leaving, I will be dead after you. You will come back to take another wife to do the work of your God there."

I asked her, "Are you going to commit suicide?"

She added, "No, but I'd rather die than stay to see such a shame."

A voice said to me, and I knew it came from God, "Let me talk to her."

And I remained silent until morning. Except I spent time in prayer. A passage from Romans 5:1–5 comforted me: "Therefore, having been justified by faith, we have peace with God through our Lord Jesus Christ, through whom also we have access by faith into this grace in which we stand, and rejoice in hope of the glory of God. And not only that, but we also glory in tribulations, knowing that tribulation produces perseverance, and perseverance, character, and character, hope. Now hope does not disappoint, because the love of God has been poured out in our hearts by the Holy Spirit who was given to us."

During morning worship at my workplace, while the thought had not left me, our friend Beingar did the reading in John 16:33: "These things I have spoken to you, that in Me you may have peace. In the world you will have tribulation; but be of good cheer, I have overcome the world." I remembered the different impacts that occurred in my workplace, like the anaphylactic reactions after giving a shot to a patient. I imagined that if it resulted in death, maybe I would be locked up. And it was going to be worse than serving God.

Two weeks later, precisely on the night of July 24 to July 25, 2004, my wife said that she was not happy with all my decisions. In 1994, there was first the promise of marriage in October, and suddenly, I decided to go to the Biblical School Esdras in N'Djamena (BSEN). As she was still delaying in Moundou, having learned this, she should have written a separation note. Unfortunately, I did not receive the so-called letter. She reminded me that if she broke with me at that time, it was even better than waiting until she arrived at other upsetting decisions, so she sincerely regretted.

I replied, "To tell someone I love you and then to tell him again I want to separate, it's paradoxical." My decision was to wait when God had changed my wife's heart, then it would be time to agree on what to do about other dimensions of divine work. My last thought was that responding alone to God's call was dangerous. It would be impossible to serve God by marrying another wife or taking care of the children without their mother. As my wife totally emptied herself, I asked her for forgiveness. After our prayer, she agreed that I could continue with the travel plan.

Having received the agreement at home following the agreement of my leaders, I had to announce the news to my collaborators of our local church and to the managers of the health center. It was a shock at my workplace after announcing my resignation, which would be soon. Mr. Masrayam, who I mentioned was the reason I got the job, planned to study ophthalmology in Senegal. As the religious sister was aware of his plan that would benefit the center upon his return, she was counting on me to replace him at his consulting office. But understanding that I too had to leave, she began to offer me the benefits, which would accompany my promotion. My conviction was sincere, so I did not give in. During the month of August, the offerings were made at the level of the churches of the south as well in those of N'Djamena. My fellow pastor Josué Kodeyimna, the student who was chosen from south of Chad, joined me at the end of the first week of September. My journey was becoming imminent, and I had to leave my wife pregnant for one month, the three children, and the two other girls with residues of provision without money in a bank account but by faith in God. I relied on these biblical passages: Matthew 19:29 says, "And everyone who has left houses or brothers or sisters or father or mother or wife or children or lands, for My name's sake, shall receive a hundredfold, and inherit eternal life." Philippians 4:19–20 says, "And my God shall supply all your need according to His riches in glory by Christ Jesus. Now to our God and Father be glory forever and ever. Amen."

    God planned everything. At the same time, Pascalin was about to go to Yaoundé to visit his brother Thierry Yamoudal. The evening of September 8, 2004, we departed by bus from Kousseri, the Cameroonian town near N'Djamena, Chad. We spent the night in Ngaoundéré. The next day at sunset, we continued the journey by train to arrive in Yaoundé. Thierry had no hesitation in welcoming us because he had no worries about financial means as he worked at the gas station, which paid better. He was the nephew of the wife of the apostle Abel (one of the ministries that recommended us for Bible College). For my part, he was the cousin of my brother-in-law under the tutelage of whom I spent my first years in N'Djamena. As the saying goes, "We were in the good hands." Later, Thierry would become an asset in my story. After resting well, we continued without a guide until Kumba in the Southwest of Cameroon, where we arrived on Saturday night. With information, we spotted the campus. The Southwest is Anglophone, like the Northwest of Cameroon. Just with the notions of English learned at school, we tried to make ourselves understood but difficult. On Sunday morning, we attended our first worship service at the Apostolic Church called Kumba I.

Fortunately for us, there was interpretation in French. At the end of the worship service, we were welcomed in a special room. The apostle Betang who was president of the association of Apostolic Churches of Cameroon encouraged us and the pastor of Kumba I, the reverend David Okposin translated. His key words that I had not forgotten were "my children stand firm in your training, and you will not be the same once you go back home." It was only after worship that we were introduced to Principal John Enow. He reminded us of the terms of the training contract. The Association of Apostolic Churches of Cameroon and Board of the Apostolic Bilingual Bible College (ABBC) had decided to pay our registration fees for three years. Books, food, travel, and other allowances were at our expense. The academic year 2004–2005 began, and it was the sixth promotion, which was called sixth batch in English. At the official opening on Thursday, September 16, 2004, President Betang, as his topic, he chose determination in his exhortation. His first text was in 2 Chronicles 2:1: "Then Solomon determined to build a temple for the name of the Lord, and a royal house for himself." He then read two more passages in Romans 13:7–8 and 2 Timothy 2:1–10. He ended up telling us, "Success is ahead of you." This term *you*, I took it in my heart that day personally.

My experience at the N'Djamena Bible School was totally different. After the morning worship by dormitory, we went out to cut grass under the direction of our class leader, who was called *prefect*. After this chore, everyone decided according to their means to get breakfast. I mentioned the means because some students fed at the restaurant and others with limited means cooked for themselves. It was not just breakfast but in terms of the food area. The courses were translated from English into French or from French into English according to the teachers of the day. The reverends Keminfe Theodore, Mambou Leonard, and Kuiessie Etienne were our teachers who taught in French and translated into English. Principal Apostle John Enow, Rev. Ngoto

Thomas, Rev. Okposin David, and several other guest speakers taught in English and translated into French. It was a way for me to learn English during those three academic years. I did not want to skip this parenthesis. Almost four or five days passed, we ate only rice and our supplies of peanuts—in other words, something else eatable but not *boule*. For those who do not know the boule, this is a type of food in Africa that is prepared in different ways. Among the Saras, our tribe, it is prepared by leathering millet flour, cassava, rice, and earth peas in the water to make it supple and sticky, then rolling it to make balls; in the English-speaking environment, it is called *fufu*. It is eaten with vegetable, fish, or meat soup.

As I mentioned the lack of this special food, my colleague said to me, "That is terrible. Not eating the boule all these days, but we're going to die."

My worries were less because living in N'Djamena single and then being separated from my wife for a few years, the absence of boule in my diet was not a problem. This first week was hard, but after that, we got used to the new way of life. However, later, we arranged to insert the boule into our food ration. The Association of Chadian Apostolic Churches did not have a fixed budget for us. The churches were collecting, and the amount received was transferred to us by Pastor Ronel Didier. The rarity of these transfers pushed us to go back home during Christmas break to raise money on my side at the capital, N'Djamena, and my friend in the south of Chad. During the Easter break, I had stayed in Kumba, but Joshua went to Yaoundé to negotiate a financial aid at the Embassy of Chad in Cameroon without a good result.

On April 23, 2005, our son Daniel was born. For him, I received the name in a dream. The first year ended and we went to Chad. It was at that time like the case of Sephora that I saw and kissed Daniel. My two and a half months spent in Chad were mostly spent raising money for our financial support. Thank God we had received financial aid from the churches, members of our families, and many volunteers.

Berndibaye, who was the host in N'Djamena of my colleague Josué, was one of the key characters to raise money. He typed the forms of request for support and helped a lot financially. The idea of looking for help everywhere on the internet or checking emails by Chad was the cause that when we returned for the academic year 2005–2006, I spent more weekends at the cybercafe. The college did not give us access to the internet, so we must pay for the hours of use. The schedule was the same, but there was less stress. Cooking was my domain, so I cooked a lot, and I did it with joy, without any whispers. One practice that helped me a lot at ABBC was fasting and prayers. I received the revelations in my dreams, but I kept for me if they were personal.

On Monday, September 19, 2005, at night, I had a dream where I was with the white officials who looked after the children. Immediately, I realized that the idea coincided with my plan to write to Carolyn, an American woman who Florence met at AGLO in 2001. It was to ask her to sponsor us so that I could continue my theological studies and Florence could work with children as she did and go and create a center for children in Chad.

Another Monday night, October 24, 2005, I had another dream. I was in the courtyard of an office of the minister. There were names displayed for theological studies. Among the beneficiaries, I clearly saw my name for a faculty in Israel (Israel for me was Europe) because it coincided with my online application for registration for the faculty at Strasbourg. Being very happy to see my name, the secretary of this office told me to hurry up to compile my dossiers. October 25, 2005, was not the weekend, but I decided to go check my emails, but there was no good message. Only, outside the cybercafe, at the entrance, the owner posted the result of the candidates who applied in 2003 to the website: www.dvlottery.state.gov. I had seen, among other countries, Chad with a very short list of beneficiaries. The list of names of people from other countries was long, even those in Cameroon. In my curiosity, I asked what these names were. Daniel, the owner, told me that these were people who applied for the American lottery in 2003 and that the result was out in 2005. It was an opportunity for lucky people to go live and work in the United States. I asked him why Chadians were so few. He told me maybe Chadians did not want to travel. I was interested and asked him if people were still doing it. He said that October was the month chosen for the application. I had returned to the campus, and every day, I prayed for divine guidance.

On Saturday, October 28, 2005, at the end of the classes, I isolated myself to pray again and went to the cybercafe. Immediately, Daniel, the manager, called his photographer friend. He took my picture and printed it in passport size. Daniel scanned the photo to attach to the application. No more than thirty minutes, the confirmation note appeared on the screen. He printed and handed it to me. As he was familiar with the application procedure, he recommended me to keep the piece of paper well and wait until May or June 2006 for the result. What he wrote in the application was my first and last name, my date of birth, my profession, and my marital status. For marital status, I wrote fiancé, as Florence and I did not have a marriage certificate from the commune. I put the address of the Bible school of Chad, as I did not have my personal post mailbox. This application I made was very reassuring, so I stopped spending too much on the internet if not just to check my emails. The year 2005–2006 was less scary because we got used to the food and teachers, as they were the same ones who continued to teach except for a few guest speakers. The college sent us to local churches for the internships on Sundays.

In one of these local churches, I met Papa Kema, who would play an important role in my journeys in the future. We had returned to Chad at Christmas break, but at Easter break, Josué had gone to the north of Cameroon with Bakary, a colleague, and I was invited to Bamenda in the northwest of the country, to Apostle Eyong Joseph's house. I preached at a conference and returned to Kumba financially blessed. During the holidays of 2006 at the beginning of June, my colleague had gone to Sarh (south of Chad) for his internship, and I had to do mine in Nguéli. Our internships were mandatory for our study agenda.

As I was present in N'Djamena, I went to Director Myalbaye David, who replaced the previous Western directors. I asked him if he had not received a letter in my name coming from somewhere. He said no. A slight despair grew in me, but my hope always remained firm.

This was the period that Daniel, who was responsible of the cybercafé, told me in Cameroon, but maybe there was a bit of delay. I did not ask for the letter again, but in August, I was passing through Esdras, and the director brought me a large envelope with this address:

Kentucky Consular Center
3505 N. Highway 25 W
Williamsburg, KY 40769 (Return Service Requested)

As I read the Kentucky, USA, address, I told him that this was the letter I asked him for in June. He apologized because at the time he received the mail, he put it together with those of the missionary who was on vacation in France. He had just returned and told him that this letter was for me. I did not blame David, but I knew that the devil was fighting God's plan in my life. To avoid allowing the devil to play more with bad thoughts in my mind, I thanked David and went home immediately. I opened the letter, and the first page put me in an inexpressible joy. So I knelt to thank God and asked him to give me wisdom for the rest of the process.

United States Department of State

Washington, D.C. 20520

Congratulations!

You are among those randomly selected and registered for further consideration in the Diversity Immigrant Visa program for fiscal year 2007 (October 1, 2006 to September 30, 2007). Please read the instructions and follow them carefully to continue processing your application. In order to help insure that all available visas are used each year, more people are randomly selected than there are visas; thus visa issuance to you cannot be guaranteed, even if you meet all the qualifications, and it is important that you complete and return the forms listed below as quickly as possible. After you return all of the forms listed below and if there are appointments available, we will schedule you for an interview at the appropriate embassy/consulate. You will be contacted by the Department of State by mail if you are selected for an interview.

Important Basic DV-2007 Requirements

The law creating the Diversity Immigrant Visa Program states that to qualify for a diversity visa, you must have either a high school education, or its equivalent, or two years of work experience. A high school education means successful completion of a formal course of elementary and secondary education comparable to completion of a 12-year course in the United States. If you are qualifying with work experience, you must have two years of experience in the last five years in an occupation which, by U.S. Department of Labor definitions, requires at least two years of training or experience. The U.S. Department of Labor provides information on job duties, knowledge and skills, education and training, and other occupational characteristics at their website http://www.doleta.gov/programs/onet/ or http://stats.bls.gov/oco/oco2007.htm. You must have either a high school education or sufficient work experience to qualify for a DV visa.

If you are qualifying with work experience, you must have two years of experience in the last five years in an occupation defined by U.S. Department of Labor as qualifying for the DV Program. The Department of Labor (DOL) O*Net Online Database http://online.onetcenter.org/ groups job experience into five "job zones." While many occupations are listed on the DOL Website, only certain specified occupations qualify for the Diversity Visa Program. To qualify for a Diversity Visa on the basis of your work experience, you must, within the past five years, have two years of experience in an occupation that is designated as Job Zone 4 or 5, classified in a Specific Vocational Preparation (SVP) range of 7.0 or higher. For more information on the DOL O'NET, refer to <http://www.doleta.gov/programs/onet/> or <http://stats.bls.gov/oco/oco2007.htm>.

If you do not meet one of these requirements, you are not eligible to be issued a diversity visa. Only you, as the principal applicant, must meet this requirement. Your spouse and children do not have to meet this requirement. Do not continue with this application if you do not meet the education or work experience requirement.

If you are scheduled for a visa interview, at the time of the interview consular officers will evaluate medical exam results, financial evidence, and police certificates. So, you must bring the original and one copy of all the documents listed in the enclosed instructions and your original notification letter to your interview. You are required to provide the consular officer with the English language translation of

An idea came to me to talk to my friend Djigueri and his Nigerian collaborator who were staying at the orphanage located outside the city of N'Djamena. Very clearly, both were not available to help me because of their multiple occupations. I left them to go home a little disappointed because the time limit was getting very short. To move faster, I used my French-English dictionary to be able to answer questions. The responses were written according to each page in the sheets. I had gone to the market and found a gentleman typing customers' texts with the typing machine. I explained to him my goal, which was to insert the words or sentences in blank spaces of my documents. To be sure of the job well done, I stayed with him all the way. He would insert each page, and manually, he could manipulate the pages from top to bottom and from left to right to find the blank spaces to fill. The work took time, but he did it impeccably. I paid for it, and without delay, I went to make photocopies. I put in the envelope the originals and went to the central post office in N'Djamena to ship to the address given in the documents. As this phase was over, I was starting to think about the passport. I spoke to my brother-in-law Eloi, the husband of my younger sister Elizabeth, who gave me 100,000 francs CFA ($200). The next day, I started the procedure, and through my police neighbor Malon, I got my passport before the end of my vacation. As the fundraising in 2006 was fruitful, I thought that the academic year 2006–2007 should be happier. But the devil orchestrated a terrible attack. In September 2006, Josué and I returned to Kumba. As it was the weekend, I took the opportunity to announce the good news of the result of my application to Daniel, the owner of the cybercafe. That was when the truth came out, and it was for my good.

He said, "Nouba, congratulations, but you were lucky. I applied three successive years, and I never had the chance, and just a first time, you were retained. Truly, your God is alive."

If he had told me about his failures before, I was not even going to try. I told him that I filled out the documents. I sent to the United States by post office before returning from vacation. He was not convinced of my mailing. So he suggested that he could scan the copies that I had to make sure Kentucky Consular had received either one or the other. I paid him the fees he charged. On Sunday, I went back to collect my copies and made sure he had managed to get the job done.

The current year, some pastors joined our batch to finish their third year as they had only done two years according to the previous curriculum. In our dormitory, they added Rengou and the others. During that night, from Sunday to Monday, something weird had happened. Rengou dreamed that a student had been attacked or killed, and he woke up his colleague to pray in the middle of the night. I remembered involuntarily the same night, going upstairs, entering the classroom, and going downstairs back to bed. In the morning, the new manual labor leader Taku Alfred made a group for cutting the grass, as we did in previous years. He put me with another student, and our portion was close to the valley that ran along the river called Kumba Water. I was in my shorts, had new slippers on my feet, and was using my new and sharp cutting tool. Barely thirty minutes passed, Taku came to call my companion to go and show him another portion that we had to cut after finishing in that first place. Continuing alone to work with my head down, suddenly, a slide took me, and I could see myself upside down going toward the hollow.

I shouted, "Jesus, Jesus!" And a force turned my legs bent, and I had fallen with my right knee and trunk on a large rock covered with previously cut grass. A student who had seen me fall was screaming, and a few students had come down to the accident site. All hoped I could get up, but I could not. Aniedi, one of the students, also arrived at the site. He put his arms under my armpits and stood me up. I tried to walk, and I was going to collapse with each attempt. I told them that I had a fracture. Seeing only the abrasions, several said that none of my bones were broken.

When I touched my right knee, I knew it was not normal. Principal John Enow and TACC President Apostle Tambe interacted in their Bayangue dialect and decided to bring me to the hospital urgently. The x-rays did not reveal anything at the level of my chest and abdomen, but my right kneecap broke into two pieces. Dr. Ojong proposed surgery to repair the fracture. I was kept in the hospital, and on the second day, I underwent surgery followed by a cast that went from the thigh to the ankle.

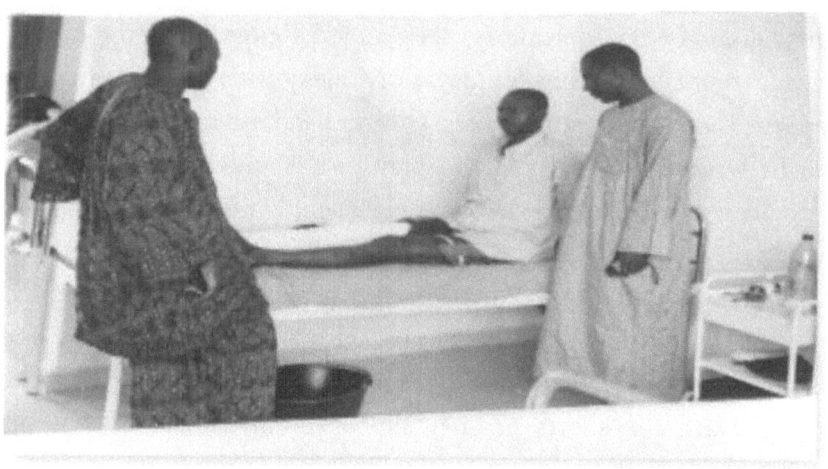

Being a few days in the hospital, I appreciated the good care of student friends, officials, and Christians. Some students slept at my bedside and had helped me with the ADLs. Our colleague Essomba, being a carpenter, made two crutches for me. Once discharged, I returned to campus. I was only going to the hospital by appointment for up to two months. X-rays were repeated to control healing. After two months, the doctor ordered that the cast should be removed. At the time of going for this appointment, I was happy to be able to be without a cast on my leg, remembering the difficulty of bathing or using the toilet. With care, the cast was removed from my leg. Trying to walk, I could not bend my right leg. I asked the doctor if my leg was going to stay like this for good. He said that rehabilitation was necessary to restore mobility. I took RV with the doctor of physical therapy (PT) in town. I paid the fees, and the rehabilitation began. The pain at first was almost unbearable. I shed bitter tears. The doctor told me that if I wanted to reuse my leg, I would have to cry and let him do his job. At this moment, I remembered the two Chadians having one of the legs that did not bend, and I imagined myself walking like them for the rest of my life. Not only the worry of being disabled, but my plan to go to the interview for an imminent immigration to the United States had generated a lot of concerns. My colleague Kamto Arsene kept telling me that I was like Joseph of the Bible (from the pit to the palace in Egypt). I was very encouraged by that. My finances and studies were disturbed, but the divine support kept me. We talked about a real attack of the devil in my life. Rengou did not stop thanking God for understanding the insight the night before the accident.

I mentioned somewhere about my integration to the state workforce. In November and December 2006, all state officials had to register. I was forced to travel in December during Christmas break to register too. The trip was arduous, but I was able to arrive in N'Djamena. The census officers understood me because of my accident. The miracle would happen during the rest of my stays. One evening, my cousin Nguewoud Riminan went to visit me, and he was on a bike. We were talking for a while, so I interrupted, and a word of faith came out of my mouth.

I told him, "I'm going to ride your bike."

I got up and put my right foot of the leg that was not bending on the pedal while standing. I sat down and started pedaling; my leg became supple and bent with the movement.

I exclaimed, "I can ride the bike!"

I did several laps before coming back to sit down. This corresponded with John's miracle in chapter 5, verse 8: "Jesus said to him 'rise take up your bed and walk.'" For this paralytic, it was to walk; for me, as I was already walking but improperly, God performed the miracle so that I could bend my leg and walk properly until now. I had no more difficulties during my return trip. My colleague Japoum Marthe, instead of glorifying God for my miracle, said that I had gone back to Chad with my wife that was why the conjugal role restored my sick leg. She said this as a joke. As I mentioned Martha's name, she was one of the three women who went to Bible College with our batch. Martha especially helped us with money and food as often as she could. She would be an unforgettable help during my family's visa application time later in Yaoundé.

As I had this accident, I was not obligated to do the manual work like others, but voluntarily, I did some with them. To mention my immigration project, every time I checked the quota if my application number was getting closer. It increased the faith in me. I told my wife to sell the land we bought in 2001 with her compensation money paid by Air France (because of 9/11). Her older sister Rachel also lent us a sum of money of 150,000 francs CFA ($300). Since I had not gone back during Easter break, she sent me some money and kept the rest. Practically, our training was coming to an end, and I had no other news; only, it seemed to me that my application number was included among those that were retained on the website: www.travel.state.gov. I did not mention one thing, but when I returned for the academic year of 2006–2007, I bought a mobile phone. As on the USCIS website, candidates were asked to do the update, if necessary; I inserted my cell phone number. At the end of May 2007, we were in final exams. I was in the middle of an exam one morning, and my phone was vibrating as I put it on Silent mode. With our situation as students, we did not want to miss phone calls because none of them would be an advertisement. I looked, and I saw the embassy in Yaoundé. I asked the supervisor's permission that I had to take this call. I walked away, and a gentleman was speaking to me in French.

He said in an English-speaking accent, "Noubaissem you will have a RV for your interview at the US Embassy in Yaoundé on June 15, 2007. You will need to bring all the requested documents to the USCIS website."

I had sat back in my place all joyful. I do not remember how I finished the exam that day. The closest friends heard the good news, then it was the camp and the teachers who knew about it. The first week of June 2007 was the preparation for the graduation ceremony.

Apostle Abel, Pastor Enoch, and two other pastors had arrived in Kumba for the event. My wife, Florence, traveled from N'Djamena in the company of the servants of God who came to assist their students in another city in Cameroon. When they separated on the way, Florence was able to arrive in Kumba, and the number reached five people who surrounded us at our graduation.

The last church where I did my internship and a Christian businesswoman, who supported us a lot and because of their friendship with Josué, committed themselves to the organization of our reception as Chadian students. This lady also hosted, fed, and financed the delegation of Chad. My wife and I had managed a place to sleep as a couple separately. Before being very busy with the end of training, I prepared the mind of Yamoudal Thierry, our friend from Yaoundé, that my wife and I would be at his house at the end of June for my interview at the embassy. The money my wife collected had been spent largely on her trip and stay in Kumba. I would hope that our leaders in Chad would give me my share of travel money as I would not immediately return with them, but they did not give me anything. However, my wife and I left the same day with the delegation of servants of God from Chad. Josué traveled with the ministers, but my wife and I stopped in Yaoundé and stayed with Thierry. Our friend's situation had changed shortly before we arrived at his house. He and his family had a decent life when he worked at the gas station. The wickedness of his bosses caused his dismissal, and he was unemployed. It was not interesting to rent a house and to feed his family being broke. Being a Christian, it was rare to see him sad. He became our guide to the procedures at the US Embassy.

Speaking of the steps, on July 2, 2007, we went to the embassy for my interview. An officer received me at the counter and took my passport to verify my identity. Then she showed me the list of recommended things before starting the interview process. The important points were the fees to be paid (165,000 CFA or $330) and the medical examinations to get done, such as chest x-ray, HIV, and TB tests (85,000 CFA or $170). She mentioned affidavit, but I was not familiar with that word. She told me that I would need to get them the name of my host in the United States. Very quickly, I gave her the name of Ramadje, the nephew of Florence. Fortunately, the nephew lived there; otherwise, I did not know anyone else. She added that my process could only begin if I brought back the results of the medical examinations and paid the fees. After explaining to Thierry and Florence, their advice was to finish with the medical examinations, go to Chad to get enough money, and come back to continue. I accepted the idea; therefore, we went home, and it was the end of the first day. As it was the weekend, my medical visit took place on Monday morning. I introduced myself to the doctor's secretary as a nurse, and this helped me to save about 10,000 francs CFA. It was a long and tiring day, but we ended it with joy. The doctor welcomed me to his office in the evening for a physical visit.

At the end of my visit, I had to see the nurse who gave me a sealed envelope and firmly forbade me to try to open it. At that moment, I remembered Adam from the Bible and the consequence of their disobedience with Eve. "Then the Lord God took the man and put him in the Garden of Eden to tend and keep it. And the Lord God commanded the man, saying, 'Of every tree of the garden you May freely eat; but of the tree of the knowledge of good and evil you shall not eat, for in the day that you eat of it you shall surely die'" (Genesis 2:15–17). The next day, Florence and I traveled to Chad. I waited two days to contact my family members during weekends. My cousin, Minister Mirangaye, gave me 100,000 francs CFA ($200), and my cousin Amina gave me 20,000 francs CFA ($40). The salaries received at this time were added, and the rest of money that my wife kept after the expenses of Cameroon allowed me to leave ten days later to go back to Yaoundé. There was no time to lose, as I no longer needed to make an appointment. In the morning, Thierry and I went to the embassy of the United States. The security asked me if I had an appointment.

I told them no. "I came to pay the fees because last time I didn't have the amount which was required."

As I approached the counter, it was another agent who greeted me. She asked me how she could help me. I told her I was coming to pay my fees. She took the money, and after counting, she cashed in and gave me the receipt. I also gave her the originals of my diplomas.

"One thing has been missing," she said. I asked her what else. She said, "You had to bring us the affidavit from your nephew whose name appeared in your profile or proof of your own bank account with enough money to live in the USA."

Thinking that it was a simple thing to get from Ramadje, I said goodbye to her, promising to come back with the necessary paper in a few days. I began to be annoyed. I was making phone calls during hours of sleep in USA without knowing it. When it was daylight in Cameroon, it was night in the United States, but I did not know. My nephew was very patient in answering me and told me that it was late hours and that he needed to rest. He sent me his citizenship certificate to prove to the embassy that he would be my host. I brought it, and the same woman told me that the document she wanted had to be called *affidavit* and not *certificate*. As I was confused, having this Chadian mentality about how strangers were welcomed, she told me that this reality was not like that of Europe or the USA. They wanted to make sure I would not be a homeless person where I was going.

"You wanted to tell me that in the whole USA, you had no one to send you the affidavit document?" she added.

Immediately, after leaving the embassy, I started making phone calls to Kumba's friends, asking them to help me find someone who could get me the affidavit. Somewhere in my writing, I mentioned the name of Papa Kema from Kumba. I did my pastoral internship for an academic year during my Bible training in the church that was in his courtyard. God directed me to call him too. He told me that one of his spiritual sons had the same opportunity being in Bible College and was in the USA. He said that the car he was driving was a gift from this spiritual son. He told me his name was John Egyawan and gave me his phone number and email address.

Respecting the right time to avoid disturbing his sleep as I did to my nephew, I sent him an email. At the normal time, I called him, and I was starting to speak English that was difficult to understand. Surprisingly, he answered me in very understandable French. I explained my situation to him, and I told him that Papa Kema gave his contact details. He assured me that he would send me the document without delay because he knew the need for the document. A few days later, I received the affidavit and went to make several photocopies, and the original, I brought to the embassy. The same agent was at the counter. When I handed her the document, she was proud of me. She said that it was an opportunity that people were looking for with tears in their eyes, and that I was going to lose it in addition with all the expenses I had already made. I thanked her for her motivation and asked when I should come back to see her. She said they had my phone number and that of my host, Thierry, so the embassy would call me if everything would be ready. It was already the beginning of August when I succeeded submitting all the documents. For my stays, I received financial support from Papa Kema, my wife, and the Apostolic Church of Odja, which was led at that time by the colleague pastor Nkono Jean Daniel. More than fifteen days went by without news from the embassy. I tried to call their number at the phone booth, but the system gave me a list of options to choose from: For security, you must press one; for the secretariat office, you must press two. And it continued. Finally, all my money was gone without saying a word. I decided not to make a phone call as I did not know which extension to choose. Thierry, being always available, accompanied me to go and find out.

Every time, I was told, "Go back home. We'll call you when your turn arrives."

I had found myself in September without realizing it. I did not know who would influence my wife, but on the phone, she expressed doubts about my situation. I was worried also because I had to be in Chad to get back to work. In mid-September, I told Thierry that I was tired of waiting. I made the decision to go and collect my documents and travel to Chad that very day. I packed my suitcase and went to the embassy. Security let me in. I sat down because there was no one at the counter. As soon as I saw an agent, I did not want to wait, when even a woman was already approaching for her information. I waited for her to finish speaking. The gentleman wanted to leave, but I intercepted him to tell him to give me all my documents today because I had no money left to keep waiting. If I stayed, I would lose my job in Chad, and I was not sure about their lottery program. He did not talk and left to talk to his boss about the woman's case and mine.

The woman said to me, 'Sir if you withdrew your files, you would no longer have the chance to apply for a visa anywhere to go to the USA next time, so think again."

The agent came back not very long after to address the woman, and I changed my mind; my files would remain, but still, I would take the train to Chad. I noticed that the woman had to wait for them a little. I approached her again to thank her. She told me her name was Mariam Kane and that she was from Kousseri (northern part of Cameroon, border to N'Djamena, the capital of Chad). As I took her number, I called her later, and she told me that she had not had her visa at that time, so I concluded that God had sent her for me. My decision, having been made, I took the train that same evening, and on the third day,

I had arrived in N'Djamena. Two days later, a phone call came from Cameroon, and it was Thierry, my host.

He said, "Pastor Nouba, the people from the US Embassy called you. They said your visa was ready. I told them you had returned to Chad, and it would take you about three to four days to come back. They told me that you could come at any time to get it."

A joy mixed with the regret for not waiting a few days animated me abundantly. I would have to look for money and travel to Yaoundé ASAP. I had arrived at my destination in the morning, I bathed, and Thierry accompanied me to the embassy. They gave me my passport with the visa for a period of six months (September 20, 2007, to March 19, 2008) to travel, and once arrived on US soil, I would have permanent resident status. In addition to the passport, I was given all the originals of my diplomas and the same sealed envelope containing the medical results. Same recommendation: "Do not open it. You will give it to custom agents at the entry airport in the United States."

The American lady who received me, pointed her finger to my degree from the Bible College, and congratulated me a lot. I thought that probably she was Christian. She told me to do my best to travel before the date of March 19, 2008, because if I did not arrive in America, my visa would expire, and it would be over for me. She wished me good luck. I thanked her before leaving. We went back, and I spent my night one last time at Thierry's. The next day, I sincerely thanked my friend and his family before returning to Chad for another three days. Once we arrived in Chad, the joy overwhelmed us, and we were truly grateful to God. On my return, I received the message from my father, telling me to do my best to visit them before traveling to the United States. I had not regretted making this trip because it was the last time for me to see him and talk to him. The enemy tried to tempt me. A thought said, "You got the visa, but where will you get a million CFA [$2,000] to pay for the plane ticket, especially since you have no savings?"

One evening, we went with my wife to my cousin, Minister Mirangaye, to show him the visa and thank him for his financial support. In my mind, it was to see if he would be excited to help again for the airfare. During this visit, I had not mentioned the need of an airline ticket, but sometime later, I went to his office talking about the situation. This time, I talked about money to borrow and repay once I would arrive in the USA. He was frank with me, and I understood him. Several of his children were studying at different universities in African countries. Taking a large sum to help me was impossible. I had repented because I had not applied the word of God. It is said in Psalm 118:8–9, "It is better to trust in the Lord than to put confidence in man. It is better to trust in the Lord than to put confidence in princes." I prayed to seek God's guidance.

On October 14, 2007, I wrote the names of thirty-five people I had to contact to borrow money. Many apologized for not being able to help me at that time. My request was for the loan, but these few people told me that they did not want to be repaid: my cousin Kadetebaye, in October 2007 (10,000 francs CFA or $20); my brother in Christ Nantoiallah and his wife, in January 2008 (50,000 francs CFA or $100); and my sister in Christ Edwige Ndangue, in January 31, 2008 (100,000 francs CFA or $200). The people who agreed to lend me were as follows: the brothers in Christ Nassarinan Tatala (100,000 francs CFA or $200) and Nanhoguinan Auguste (100,000 francs CFA or $200); my cousin Dainal and her husband, Aingongue, in November 2007 (50,000 francs CFA or $100); Servant of God Kidalbaye Djoguinan, in January 2008 (100,000 francs CFA or $200); my wife's niece Jocelyne Ousmane, in January 1, 2008 (350,000 francs CFA or $700); the older brother of my wife, Djassiara Benoudjita, in January 30, 2008 (450,000 francs CFA or $900); and finally, on February 6, 2008, my maternal aunt Christine (50,000 francs CFA or $100). You found that these sums of money were received practically close to March 2008, which would be the end of my visa.

During these races for financing, I also had to do everything to get the marriage certificate. My request was initiated, and the date chosen was Thursday, January 31, 2008, instead of Friday or Saturday because we just needed to sign the marriage certificate without any ceremony. As I will tell you, the birth of a fifth child was certainly during the two months after my return, when my wife got pregnancy. I no longer thought of finding work in Chad, but cautiously, I asked for a leave of absence from the Ministry of Health. These precautionary measures meant that everything was still hidden because no one, to my knowledge, had this opportunity to allow me to learn from their experience. Speaking of lack of experience, I inquired about airlines, and my cousin Ernestine put me in touch with Kiki Sackal, a cousin on her mother's side, who was working at Air France. God guided me in killing two birds with one stone on January 31, 2008. At the indicated time, we presented ourselves to the commune. The witnesses were punctual, except for one person on Florence's side. Fortunately, Djidainan, one of their cousins, was present, so he replaced the one who was absent.

Once finished with the marriage certificate procedure, my wife and I went to Air France because I did not want to risk that a dishonest thief would steal the money borrowed for my trip. I introduced myself to Kiki from Ernestine, her cousin. She and her colleague looked for the best option for me, and they made me the reservation for Saturday, February 9, 2008. They explained to me that my money was not enough to pay for the connection from New York the entry airport to Denver at Ramadje's, which was to be my destination. For cautious motive, I had gone to see Rimtebaye, the one who was my friend at the bridal ceremony at the church, so he contacted Raoul, his cousin who lived in New York to welcome me on arrival. I was happy with everything that was like a dream coming true step-by-step.

Chad was experiencing times of military conflict, and this was not new to any Chadian. All the time, radio or television news would announce sporadic attacks in the east or north of the country. This time, it was no longer the kind of news to ignore; the rumors ran everywhere that the rebels were coming to N'Djamena to overthrow President Idriss Deby. It was a well-prepared coup, so they won victory in all the cities of resistance and were ready to enter the capital. On Saturday, February

2, 2008, the attacks were in N'Djamena. The French army intervened fiercely, but as the elements were already in the city, they sought refuge throughout the city. The fight continued to be intense for almost three successive days. The population of N'Djamena was in disarray. Many families took refuge in Kousseri, Cameroon, and others went to the south of the country. Matthieu Benoudjita, my wife's younger brother, lived in Bongor, a town tending toward southern Chad but close to N'Djamena. My wife and I decided that she, the children, and the other members of our family should leave to join Matthew and that I had to stay alone at home to take care of the effects. During the troubles, people took advantage of stealing and destroying.

As the family left, I had the idea to spend my daytime at Djimtamra's, an elder of the church in the Walia district, which was considered less dangerous. On Tuesday evening, calm returned a little, and someone said that the French military helped expatriates to travel by military plane. On Wednesday, I went to their camp by bike, taking my passport with the US visa. Having seen them everywhere on the war vehicles and on the walls, I dropped my bike a few meters away and approached them without fear. "For God has not given us a spirit of fear, but of power and of love and of a sound mind" (2 Timothy 1:7). A French soldier, seeing me unarmed, came to me. He asked me what I was looking for. I told him that I had to travel on February 9 to the United States as a permanent immigrant, but the airport was closed because of the war. I also learned that they gave transport to those who left for Europe, so was it possible that they could help me get to Paris and make my connection to New York on the due date? He frankly told me that they favored only expatriates but not a new immigrant like me, and I was not American. To be nice, he told me to go to the airport to investigate when they were going to open it again.

With the same boldness, I went to the airport. Government soldiers were everywhere. In the same way, I parked my bike and went to those who were sitting in the shade. As usual, the superiors always sat down, and they were the ones who understood a little French. My spoken

Arabic was not good enough to talk about serious things. I explained to one of them, saying that I made the reservation to travel on February 9 to the United States, but the airport was closed there. Could he tell me when it would be open again? He said he did not know either, but he allowed me to go and talk to the officers in the office that maybe they would have accurate information for me. I went to the office, and the agents told me that they did not have an exact answer for me, but they doubted very much that the opening would take place before February 9. I thanked them and got on my bike to go home to my uncle Apostle Leon's house to explain my situation and ask him to support me in prayers. You are not going to believe it, but I could not communicate with my family anymore.

Fortunately, Florence's absence helped me to take these steps on this day. Because if she was in N'Djamena, she was not going to let me go. It was a risk I took, but God and his angels protected me. Remaining alone at home, I received the visit of Hervé, a young man from my church. He was the boyfriend of Hilaria, the niece of my wife who also went to Bongor. He asked me how my day was and if I got news of the family. For the family, I said that I did not have any news as all phone connection was cut off and no one came back from their side. I also explained to him the risk I took to find out about my trip. He was like a prophet sent by God. He told me that he informed his relative Yobom, who was also my friend. Both were concerned that the airport was closed right after I made my reservation.

Then he added, "Yobom said you could travel from any African airport by Air France if you made the change of departure place in your plane ticket."

I immediately received this information as a prophecy of God. There was no telephone network yet to allow me to communicate with my family, so I did not wait for my wife's opinion. The idea of going to Yaoundé came to mind strongly. Entrusting everything to God in my prayers at night, I only followed the flow of divine direction on the day of February 7, 2008. I took my bike and went to Ernestine my cousin's house to help me meet Kiki to negotiate the option of changing the plane departure location. When I entered the courtyard, my cousin came from outside. I told her it was my chance thinking she had just gone out. No, it was rather a favor of God because she said that a couple days ago, she and her cousin Kiki had found refuge in Kousseri, Cameroon.

"I decided to come to check my home and go to Kiki's to check hers and go back to Kousseri," she said.

Let us imagine that if this miracle had not happened, what should I do? I left my bike at her house after explaining everything to her. We took the motorcycle taxi to go to Kiki's, we checked her home, then we continued to Apostle Leon's house to inform him of my program because he was my uncle, and he was the first leader of the Apostolic Churches of N'Djamena. As I said before, I was pastor of one of the Apostolic Churches, and I was going to be absent once again, so he should be aware. After all this tour, we continued to Guéli, a Chadian town border of Kousseri, with the same motorcyclist. I paid for the ride, and we continued to Kousseri by bus. When I saw the number of refugees, I told my cousin Ernestine, "But how I could find her among this crowd of totally unknown people?"

We went to find Kiki. When I saw her, I went right to the point. I had come so that she could call the Air France agency of Cameroon to change my travel departure place. As the phone call required the calling card, I bought an amount that would help make a long conversation. She began by calling the Douala branch. She insisted, but no one responded. Afterward, she tried in Yaoundé; immediately, the agent replied. She introduced herself as a colleague at the Chad agency before talking about my situation. The gentleman said that it was possible to make the change at the office in Yaoundé. Kiki asked me if I would be able to travel on the same day to maintain the date of February 9; that way, I would not add any other fees. By faith, I said yes, I could travel. Immediately, I went back to N'Djamena because the time was already tending toward afternoon. I took my luggage and went to Hervé's house to give him the keys to keep them for my family. I had gone back to Apostle Leon because he promised to bring me to Kousseri if the negotiation was successful. Once he saw me, he prayed for me, and we left. I finished the formalities at the border office, and he took me to the bus station. I was not worried because I used to travel on the same route for the last three years. I only had a medium suitcase and other handbag for my documents. We practically took off around 4:00 p.m. on that day.

Not far after Kousseri, the control began. The officers sent all the passengers away. All of them went back in the bus, but they stopped me because I was Chadian. Since there was war in my country, they said that I was fleeing with a ton of money going into exile. They had scattered everything in my suitcase on the ground, but they could not find anything.

To force things, they told the driver to take off and leave me if I would not pay at least 5,000 francs CFA or $10. You will say that it is little money, but it was enough for the next travel expenses. I paid to avoid the worst because if I stayed with them, they could even kill me and take everything (my passport and the little money I had in my pocket). We had arrived in Maroua, and I shipped the mobile phone to Ernestine, who was still in Kousseri, to give to my wife. That was where I was able to eat a little. After this little rest time, we continued without another long stop to Ngaoundéré. I spent the rest of the night at the bus station. In the morning, I went to sleep at Ngaoundéré pastor's house because my next departure would be in the evening by train to Yaoundé. We took the train on the evening of February 8, 2008, to enter Yaoundé on February 9 in the morning. Once I got out of the terminal, I intercepted a taxi driver and asked him to go to Odza and continue to the Air France agency, which was better, or go to Air France first before going to Odza. (Odza was the neighborhood where the church of Pastor Jean Daniel, my colleague, was located.) The taxi driver was nice and advised me to stop at Air France first.

I told him, "Well, please take me to the Air France agency."

It was not very far from the terminal; I could even walk there if I knew before. I got out from the taxi right in front of the office, so I went in. The first employee who saw me at the door asked me what I was looking for. I told him that I had come to change my place of departure for my trip to the United States. I tell you that I was really surprised by his look of denigration.

He asked me, "Where did you say?" As if he had not heard the first time.

And I repeated, "To the United States." I was dirty, dehydrated, and even hungry, without a suit on me, so he doubted I was telling the truth. As we were talking in the lobby, he told me to enter a room near us to see the chief. I introduced myself and told the man inside that I had been sent by Kiki from Chad. Luckily, it was the same agent, so he knew my situation. He took my passport and changed the place and time of departure, which was 9:00 p.m. (local time). I thanked him very much and went out. Without delay, I took the taxi to go to Odza, to Pastor Jean-Daniel's. The pastor was at a pastoral meeting. However, the young guy I met called him on the phone to inform him about my presence at his house. I could call him before I arrived, but I did not have his phone number. Between Africans, it did not matter, and my stop at his house would only be for half a day. As I had the rest of the money still in our currency, I decided to convert it into dollars after I bathed and changed clothes. I did not need a guide because my three-month stay in Yaoundé to wait for the visa allowed me to know the essential places, like the central market I was going to. I made the exchange of money, and I went back; in the meantime, the pastor was already at home. As he was waiting for me to eat, we had gone to the dining table. I told him to look for a taxi that would take me to Nsimalen, Yaoundé International Airport.

He told me, "Pastor, don't worry, I asked our church's elder Mr. Noupa to give you ride, and he agreed. In addition, Moujefou Jean Daniel, one of my youth group members from the church, would be at work at the airport tonight, so he would guide you for the rest of the formalities."

As in the African term, I said, "Weeeh, Pastor, may God bless you abundantly."

When the elder arrived at the indicated time, in unity, they prayed for my trip. After the prayer, we went without delay to the airport. From outside, Noupa called the other Jean Daniel, the airport employee, who came hastily to join us. The elder and the pastor walked with me until the area forbidden to the companions. They wished me a safe trip, I thanked them, and they left. I was not new to my guide as he had already met me. He led me step-by-step to do the formalities by introducing me to the agents as a pastor. We finally arrived at the waiting room, and he left me there while advising me to listen to the departure signal. I also thanked him for all he did for me. I watched the movements of the other passengers, and as all were heading toward an entrance, I followed them. It was my first trip by plane. I thought we had to walk or take the bus to get on the plane as I saw people doing in Chad. To my surprise, where we went was already the entrance of the plane. I looked for my seat as indicated in the ticket and sat down. Instructions for safety were given; shortly after, I felt the movement of the plane. I began to combine thanksgiving with the cry of joy. We were in the air, but in a short flight time, we landed. I was confused, and when I asked what was wrong, I was told that we stopped in Douala to pick up the other passengers. Once they had boarded the plane, the journey continued. At my side, two men sat down, I was sure they were also amazed because I did not look like them.

They asked me where I was going, and I said, "To the United States." Curiously, they wanted to know why. If it was for a visit or studies. I answered again that it was to live there because I had won the American lottery. The questions stopped, but I kept listening to their conversation, and they said that some people are lucky. They named their acquaintances who tried several times without success. Soon after, the hostesses began to serve delicious dishes. I ate it, and

I was completely full. Being tired, I fell asleep, and when I woke up, it was at our approach to Paris when we were told about the safety measures to be taken. When I got off the plane, I followed the others and the orientations of the guides who were at the airport. At the customs control, they discovered in my suitcase the pair of scissors and the needle with the sewing string, and they obliged me to throw them in the trash. They carefully checked my documents and directed me to the waiting area.

A white lady sat next to me, and I started talking to her about Jesus. She was not really interested in my conversation, and eventually, she got away from me. During the conversation, I forgot to listen to the announcements. A little bit before noon, I heard my name, and the person said that it was a last call; if I would not show up, my departure would be with the next flight. I ran to the place where the message was coming from. Some officer checked my passport and told me to run fast in the direction he was pointing to. Quickly, I arrived, and as in Yaoundé, it was the entrance of the plane. I settled in my seat as indicated in the ticket. After running out of breath, I told myself that God made me avoid these unnecessary worries because I was doing his business. "And He said to them, 'Why did you seek Me? Did you not know that I must be about My Father's business?'" (Luke 2:49).

Many people were in the Boeing plane from Paris to New York. The announcements were given in French and then in English, so I still understood everything they said. In the same way as from Cameroon to France, they served food on the plane; therefore, I expected positively to eat more from Paris to New York. The ride was long, so I slept enough. I dreamed of traveling on a bus, and I saw the trees spinning as being in movement due to the speed of the bus. When I woke up, I did not understand anything because it did not make sense because I was on the plane. On February 10, 2008, in the afternoon, New York time, we arrived. I followed the line for control at the port of entry of the United States. It was a long process. I gave them the sealed envelope. The officers took me to a different place to fill out several documents.

I picked up my suitcase, thinking it was over, but I had to go through the customs service to check what I had at the entrance of the US. As I was allowed to go out to the place of reception of guests or newcomers, I walked with the crowd.

A white lady named Aouda approached me. She spoke to me in English, and since it seemed to her that I did not answer, she decided to speak in French. She asked me if anyone was present to welcome me. I told her that my brother Raoul had to be somewhere to wait for me. The term *brother* in Chad is common; it does not necessarily mean that someone has the same father and mother as you. Since there was apparently no one waiting for me, the lady used her money to call Raoul at the number I gave her in a phone booth. There was no answer. (The big brother Raoul later told me that he was in a different airport waiting for me.) Aouda also called my nephew Ramadje's phone number in Denver and John Egyawan's number to allow me to talk to them. In my trouble, I was going to forget the promise made to them. Although I received the affidavit from John, my plan was to live with Ramadje. I asked John to tell me his position so I could go to his house. It was stupid because I was no longer in Chad, where I arrived at people's homes during my previous adventures without informing them. My friend John reminded me of what was agreed.

Not knowing what to do and since Aouda could not waste all her time for me, she asked me if I had the money for the connection to Denver. I told her that I only had $160. She said that if I wanted, she would put me on a bus, and after two days, I would get to my destination. When she said that, I remembered the dream I had on the plane. I accepted the idea, and she took me down the road, and immediately, a bus stopped. She called a young man by name and told him to take care of me until the traveling bus station. I saw the vehicles running on roads one above the other. I talked to myself, "Where was I finally?"

The bus stopped somewhere, and the young man told me to give him $3, although I had already paid for transportation on the bus. I did not argue, and I gave him the money. We walked a little while, and something white fell on us. Without asking him, I knew that it was the snow that the Bible mentioned: "White as snow." Advancing a little further, we went down the stairs lower than the previous level. I prayed internally for protection. Turning behind a building, I saw several buses parked. He guided me to a driver and explained my situation to him. After he told me that his mission was over, I thanked him, and he left. The driver told me to go pay at the counter, and they charged me $100.

The departure was announced, and the passengers had boarded. My bag was not big, so I kept it with me. We stopped at one bus station, and Moussa Abba, a Muslim from West Africa who lived in Philadelphia, joined us. He understood that I was a newcomer. He asked me where I came from. Eventually, we became friends for a long distance. He gave me his mobile phone to call my nephew Ramadje to tell him my situation and my arrival time according to the information that I got initially. They did not serve food on the bus as on the plane. I was starting to get hungry and cold. At the next stop, I saw people line up to buy either chips, other snacks, or soft drinks. I asked the driver if there was no restaurant around. He showed me a place not far from the station. And I went there. I read the menu, and I saw chicken noodle soup. I knew the chicken, which was *poulet* in French and the word *soup*, which was also the same in French with *e* at the end. Noodle was a new word to me, but both words were important: *chicken* and *soup*. I asked for the price and was told it was $5, I paid, and I was served food in a disposable bowl. When I took the bowl, I saw things, like spaghetti, that I could easily count how many were floating in a hot liquid without any meat. I grabbed it with both hands and went out without saying anything. I drank the liquid, and its heat ran all along my digestive system. I drank everything and ate the few noodles, and suddenly, the cold disappeared.

The journey resumed, and we arrived in St. Louis, Missouri, on February 12, in the evening. The driver told us that we could not continue because of snowstorm. I put my suitcase in a corner and used it as a pillow to sleep that night. In the morning, an elderly lady named Mrs. Stevenson Gracie accompanied her son who came to travel with us. The son was not interested in me, but his mother approached me and asked me questions. We chatted a little, and she gave me $5 to have coffee. I thanked her because I was going to use my own money for my breakfast.

Without delay, the bus took off, and the bus stopped at each station as we were traveling. It was night, but we were continuing our trip. Finally, as the drivers always announced the places where he had to stop to prepare the minds of the passengers, I heard Denver, and I said inwardly that this would finally be my destination. The driver parked, I took my bag, and once I entered, I saw the time, and it was 11:30 p.m. on February 13, 2008. (A kind of recap: February 7, 2008, by bus, from Kousseri to Ngaoundéré; February 8, by train, from Ngaoundéré to Yaoundé; February 9, by plane, from Cameroon to France; February 10, by plane, from Paris, France, to New York, USA, because of the time zone; and February 10–13, 2008, by bus, from New York to Denver.)

My last communication with Ramadje was at St. Louis with Gracie's phone, and I did not know when we were going to arrive, so he could not come to wait for me at the bus station. I saw a man in security uniform. I asked him to call my nephew. He dialed the number that I gave him, and as it was ringing, he handed me the phone. I told Ramadje that I had arrived at the Greyhound Bus Station in Denver. Since Ramadje lived for about ten years in Denver, he knew the place. In less than forty-five minutes, I saw them coming with another Chadian friend, Aristophane. They took me, and we went to Ramadje's house. Although it was late, I ate and took a bath before going to bed tired. Two successive days, I only slept and got up to eat and to bathe. On the third day after my arrival, I regained enough strength. Aristophane, who I mentioned, lived with his uncle Gustave. At that time, as I joined them, we were only the four Chadians, but the other friends were from different African countries. There were some Chadians before me, but they had moved to other places.

Very quickly, the good things began to come. On February 14, 2008, I received my Social Security card, and few days later, they sent me my green card. Being in possession of these essential documents on February 27, Ramadje took me to get my identification card. Since I had all the legal documents, I told my nephew to help me find work. We tried the home health service, and the manager told me that I had not even been here three months; also, I did not have the US nursing license, so she could not hire me. Totally disappointed, we went back home. I was beginning to see the importance of making sure of getting a specific host before coming to the United States.

Ramadje decided to take me to Express Services Inc., which was a company that offered temporary jobs. They recruited me, and the next day, they called me and asked me to go to Aurora's Home Depot the next morning to work. I was very excited but did not know where the Home Depot was. Luckily, Tonya, an acquaintance of Ramadje, gave me a ride. I went to the counter, and they put me under the supervision of a man. The gentleman gave me a paint, a brush, and a towel; he showed me a space to paint. I had a father who was a mason, but I had not helped in painting, at least in a professional way, in my whole life. I spent my first day to do just this work, but the outcome was not appreciated. I noticed, but the man had not mentioned anything. At the end of the day, I asked if I would come back to the same place, and the gentleman told me to contact the agency who had sent me. I went out thinking that my ride was somewhere, and I did not see anybody. I had gone back inside to talk to the people at the counter; they took pity on me and gave me $10 to take the bus.

By the information that I received, I spotted the bus station, and a driver told me which bus was going to my direction. The few outings with Ramadje allowed me to know the key landmarks toward the direction of his home. I arrived home at sunset. In the morning, I called my company, and the secretary told me that they had a job in another place for me. It was not that morning but the next day. I printed the itinerary of the new place, and I asked questions to people; fortunately,

I found it without a problem. This time, I was put with an African American. The bosses of this place wanted to free up a large space for their project and asked us to move all the things that occupied this place to another place. (There were boards, iron bars, furniture, etc.) My comrade thought that we were going to work at his pace, and that next day, we should come back to continue. I had not read my colleague's mind, and I worked hard to gain the trust of my agency when they were going to receive my report. We had moved all the stuff in one day.

At the end, while walking to the bus station, my comrade told me that he had never done such a heavy job in his life in a day. I was tired that day. Anyway, in the morning, I called the agency again; the secretary told me that she had nothing for me now, but she promised to call me when she would receive an offer.

CULTURE SHOCK

I am going to take this time to talk about my culture shock. My nephew lived in a condominium where there were neighbors next to him and downstairs. I had not seen any of them for a few weeks. Once I saw one of the neighbors, my nephew only made a quick introduction, and that was it.

During my first days, the nephew told me about an American student named Nathanaël Tishman who volunteered for the peace corps in Chad in the past. They had met at the University of Denver (UD), and at that moment, he took his phone number. I called the gentleman, as he was excited to meet me; he invited me to a cafeteria near UD. I talked about my temporary job done in town, so my appointment with Nathaniel had to follow the same day after moving heavy stuff, so I came back home hungry. The way in which guests were invited to Chad, the host had to cook everything, but if it would be in a restaurant, likewise, the host would decide to pay for everything, and if the guest would try to participate, the host, in his pride, would say no by saying that it was he or she who had invited you, the guest. Not having a ride that day, I had walked to go to this appointment, and fortunately, I had $5 in my pocket. As Nathanaël was waiting for me outside, as soon as I arrived, he understood without hesitation that it was me, and he began to speak to me in French. We entered and sat down. Knowing enough about the geography of Chad, he asked me where I lived in Chad. I told him about my birthplace, which was Sarh, then I added that I lived my last years in N'Djamena, the capital of Chad.

After these opening questions in our conversation, he told me that he ordered a latte, and he asked, "You, what were you going to order?"

I told him I only had $5, so maybe just a cup of black coffee was what I would be able to afford. What pushed me to speak like this was because of my stays in Cameroon; no one expected that the friend would pay you even if it was he who invited you to eat. For Nathanael, who lived in Chad, I was surprised that he did not tell me that he would be the one who had to pay. He had immediately called the manager to bring my cup of black coffee. I chose to be joyful because I had met him, and we had talked for a long time. As soon as he realized that it was time for him to return to the campus, he expressed his pleasure to meet me and wished me goodbye. We each paid for what we consumed, and we separated. Since then, I realized that the culture would no longer be Chadian for the rest of my life.

Another shock was that in my walking in town, I met black pedestrians like me, and I always tended to greet them, but they did not answer me. Later, I found a permanent job and a different kind of attitude shocked me a lot for a long time before getting used to it. A colleague could arrive after you at work, but he or she would not say good morning or good evening. Sometimes, these people would be at work before you and you would say hello, but they would not dare answer you. The habit in Chad was different; if someone did not greet you or respond to your greeting, you were enemies, unless the person had not heard you or had not seen you. It could happen, so if it happened once or twice, it was tolerable; but if it was continuous, it meant something did not go well between these people.

Another point: We knew some family members, and they lost their mother. We went there at the funeral, and other people asked us if we knew the deceased since we came and gave our condolences. This was a question that would never be asked in Chad. Unless a person was accused of being the perpetrator of the death, as a security measure, he could not come to the funeral. But everyone knew that if someone was present at the funeral, it was because the person knew the deceased or a member of his or her family.

More examples of culture shock: Someone wants to give you something or help you. This person tries to beg you to accept their offer or donation. A college professor friend named Dan wanted to help my family financially; not only him, but several other people from the church and friends who knew me at work were begging me to take what they wanted to give to my family financially or materially. Finally, I understood that individualism was in full swing in the United States, and I concluded that people refused offers from others because of pride or they did not want to hear from these people that it was they who helped them. I refer to the Bible because every good thing someone does deserves reward from God or from men. It says in Matthew 6:2–4 (NKJV),

> Take heed that you do not do your charitable deeds before men, to be seen by them. Otherwise, you have no reward from your Father in heaven. Therefore, when you do a charitable deed, do not sound a trumpet before you as the hypocrites do in the synagogues and in the streets, that they may have glory from men. Assuredly, I say to you, they have their reward. But when you do a charitable deed, do not let your left hand know what your right hand is doing, that your charitable deed may be in secret; and your father who sees in secret will Himself reward you openly.

The list continues: Someone you know may be sick, and they refuse your sympathy. Although he suffers, but he will tell you not to worry about him or her. It happened to me that a friend, from a different room in the house, had stayed in his room for two days in a row. Other people were asking me for his news. I was embarrassed, but I replied that I had not seen the person for two days. I had come home and knocked on his door to ask what was wrong. He got angry and told me that for two days, he was not sleeping, and he had just barely gained some sleep, and I woke him up. I was surprised, but that day, I learned a lesson. No one expected attention from the other. Anyone who has read the beginning of my book will recall that I gave the example of my own father who usually did not stay in bed in the morning but decided to stay in bed one day, not wanting to come out to see if any of us would be curious to check what was wrong with him. I did it, and he blessed me. I checked on the neighbor because something might have happened to him, and the police would ask me questions that I would not be able to answer. There were many other situations, but I do not want to say them because I have gotten used to it, and it is no longer a shock for me after living for more than a decade in the USA.

JOB SEARCH AND FIRST PERMANENT JOB

Let us go back to my job search. Through my nephew's workplace and library, I had access to the computer to do a job search. The Express Services agency did not call me for work anymore. I had not gone to claim my two days' salary because the nephew fed me very well, so I was hoping to work more to earn enough money to be able to help with food. One day, I was walking to the house along Florida Avenue in Denver. I saw two men working with a large machine. I approached them and talked to the younger one because the older one was focusing a lot on his machine. I told the young one that I was looking for work, so I asked if they could hire me. The youngster, without even consulting his colleague, told me that they were employees but that he could give me the phone number of Dan, who was their boss, so I could talk to him. I wrote the number, and quickly, I went home.

I called the phone number, and the person asked me directly if I spoke Spanish. I said no, but rather, I spoke French. He told me that he did not understand French. He asked me to speak softly and calmly. I told him that I met two of his employees and asked them to hire me, and they referred me to him. As it was the weekend, he gave me an RV on Monday, March 24, 2008, at 9:00 a.m. at the same place where I met his employees. As my program was to go back and cook, after the conversation, I started cooking. When the nephew returned from his work, I told him the good news. The gentleman had not told me yet that he would hire me, but in my heart, I applied Hebrew 11:1 (NKJV): "Now faith is the substance of things hoped for, the evidence of things not seen."

On Monday morning, I showed up before 9:00 a.m. with the documents he asked me to bring. Thirty minutes later, I saw a bearded man parking his big truck. When he saw me, he knew directly that I was his future employee. We introduced ourselves to one another. He also told me the name of their company, which was D & D Utility and Construction Services. Then he took my documents and checked them. Without paying attention to the documents, he wanted to listen to my story. While telling him my story, I also mentioned my three years at the Bible College in Cameroon. He was excited to tell me that he was a Christian like me. The questions about my qualifications seemed to cause my ineligibility. He asked me if I knew anything about electricity, phone cables, etc. I said no.

"It wasn't a problem," he said.

After he said that, I was hired, but my job for this moment was to dig two to three feet each place that they would show me. These holes would indicate to them the depth of the electrical and telephone wires because at the time of drilling with the large machine, I saw there while pointing at it, the driller could not hit or cut these wires. I told him he should not worry because I would do an impeccable job. He called the oldest employee and confided me with him, and immediately, Boss Dan left. My new team leader told me that they were changing places. There was the backhoe and his big truck. He thought I knew how to drive. I hesitated to drive the backhoe, but he told me that it was easy.

One thing I had not mentioned was that I only learned to drive once in my life. It was in N'Djamena. I paid thirty minutes of learning for 1,000 francs CFA ($2). The driver showed me how to start the car and maintain first gear to do about four laps around the soccer field. It was the only car driving I had done all my life, and here I was at the first hour of my work, which had to be permanent. I was not wise to say no to a high risk. Starting the backhoe was easy, and it did not require going backward. He took the lead with the truck. I had to follow him, but as I looked down to see where to put my foot, I had not controlled his gestures (what he did or did not) to imitate him. I accelerated, and the backhoe was moving slowly. In front of me, there was the stop sign. Therefore, I was supposed to stop; on other hand, I did not want to look down again to locate the brake pedal. As I was not driving fast, I thought that it was useless to stop at the sign before continuing.

A few meters farther, my manager noticed the very serious mistake I made. He carefully pulled over his truck and told me to stop; luckily, I was able to do so. He walked to come to me. He told me to take the passenger seat, and he had driven to the new place, which was only a few blocks from the first place. For an hour, I only felt remorse for what had just happened on my first day; as no one mentioned it, I had peace. The rest of the first day went well. My boss Dan showed up, and he gave me a ride home. The work continued at this same place for a few days, so I could go there by bicycle. At the beginning of April, I asked for permission one morning to go take the written test for a driver's license. I passed the test because it was my second attempt. For the job, we had to change the site of operation, and my boss Dan would come in the morning to give me a ride and to bring me back home at the end of the day. When I told Ramadje's friends that my boss was giving me a ride back and forth, they were amazed and said, "Unbelievable. Here in America, a boss decided to drive you to your workplace back and forth." They told me that I was lucky, but I saw it rather as the grace of God in my life.

Tending toward the end of April, Dan told me that their company had gotten a contract in Gunnison, a mountain area. He asked me if I wanted to go with them. Without hesitation, I said yes for several reasons: the difficulty of looking for job and the grace of meeting him and with everything he was doing for me. I did not say it, but he even invited me one Sunday to their church in Castle Rock. As my mind was prepared, I announced to my nephew, who was also happy for the blessings that had been flowing in my life since I arrived at his house.

Precisely, on May 3, 2008, we left for Gunnison. One thing my boss Dan did not warn me about was that it was a very cold place we were heading to. Gunnison was the main town in the valley, but the team had instead settled in Almont, a small town located ten miles from Gunnison and between Crested Butte and Gunnison.

The house was big, and I was given a room for myself. A few days later, the number of workers increased. There were some employees that did not last, but most people were permanent for the duration of our contract from May until November 2008. It was a mixture of Mexicans and Caucasians, among whom I was the only black from Africa. The sites of our work were in Crested Butte, around Almont and Gunnison. Bosses and some employees went home every weekend. Sometimes, two or three employees did not travel, and this erased my worries.

As I could not find a ride to go to church, I worshiped alone at the house. By God's grace, at the beginning of June, one of the drivers did not want to go home one weekend. I asked him to drive me in the morning to Rocky Mountain Christian Ministries Church (RMCM), which was at Gunnison's exit on the road to Almont. As I did not know the opening time of this church, I told him to drop me off at 9:00 a.m., and he agreed. In the morning, he brought me. When we arrived, there was only one car. A man was getting out of it, I approached him, and I introduced myself. He introduced himself John Clement, the pastor of the church, and immediately, he welcomed me. I said goodbye to my driver because he was not willing to attend the service like I did. Half an hour later, the church was filled. I had the opportunity to meet Karen Clement, the pastor's wife; Annie, the youth pastor; and other Christians. I was the only black man during the service. Christians were really welcoming, and I felt at home because practices like the use of musical instruments and hand clapping during worship were familiar to me. The teaching was also according to biblical scriptures. At the end of the service, we were in line for snack and coffee. Mr. Larry, also known as Chief, was a member of the church and lived in Almont. The pastor asked him to give me a ride back to my place, and he was happy to do so. To the surprise of my coworker, I was home without calling him to take me.

Mr. Gary Haney, another member of the church, would also give me a ride on Wednesdays for another evening meeting. Later, not only them, but by occasion, other people gave me rides during all my stays in Almont because I had not yet learned to drive after my success in the driving written test. The vehicles were full at our camp, but I was unable to drive them myself. A short time after I was integrated into the church, I became an usher under the leading of Gary. In Psalm 84:10, it says, "For a day in Your courts is better than a thousand. I would rather be a doorkeeper in the house of my God than dwell in the tents of wickedness."

On July 21, 2008, Grace was born, and when I announced the news at the church, Barbara, a member and nurse, asked me if she could ask the women of the church to send formula for the newborn. I told her that my wife breastfed, and if the natural milk needed a supplement, it would be with the powdered milk bought locally. Once more, I could not be present at the birth of my third child out of the five that God had given us.

The stay allowed me to build a friendship that continues until these days with Dan's mother. She had gone to visit us; I did not know what to give her as a gift. If it were in Chad, I would catch or buy a rooster and slaughter it for her meal. I saw a few people doing it, so I went to buy a bouquet of roses. Her name is Rose, so I called her Maman Rose.

"I have nothing to give you but only these flowers for your welcome."

She said it was her favorite kind of flowers. As I said, until these days, our friendship continues; she is my friend on Facebook, and every year, she sends me beautiful handmade Christmas cards.

    The company ran by Dan and Don that came from the Denver area with the name D & D Utility and Construction Services changed its name in October 2008 and became Backwoods Utilities; this time, it was led by Dan Cunningham and William Lang. Both liked and appreciated my hard work, and they decided to increase my salary per hour from $9 to $10.

    Despite this salary, I paid the maximum debts made in Chad, and I helped my family and other people in Chad and Cameroon financially. The effort to pay off debts and help people from far and near was a good start. I later discovered that my income was spent largely in these two areas. I continued to pray to God that the windows of heaven would open wide bless us abundantly so that I would eliminate the debts of mortgage, student and personal loans, and credit cards. Instead, I would have a lot of money to help churches and the underprivileged (orphans and widows). The pastoral work in Chad, for which I decided to go to Bible College to improve, was replaced by the testimony of Jesus shared with all the people whom God had placed before me at my workplaces and in private life.

Always trying something new things was part of my life. It was then that I decided to register for the Pharmacy Technician program. (The institution sent me the books for the courses and homework to answer and send back by mail for grading. I did this course to finish later in December 23, 2008. This initiative pushed me to open my own mailbox in Almont. There were several reasons for this program: to learn English through reading lessons and homework, to have something that occupied me instead of keeping company with friends who spoke Spanish most of the time, and finally, to have a diploma for an eventual different job.)

God was planning another job for me. Tom, a nurse working at the Senior Care Center (SCC Nursing Home) understood in my conversations that I preferred to work in the health system, and he suggested the job of certified nurse assistant, as their center provided on-site training. Not being sure of myself, I told him to wait. Toward the end of October, the cold was starting, and Boss Dan informed me that very soon, the snow would prevent us from working outside. His plan was to take me and even to give me a place to stay in Castle Rock instead of joining my Nephew Ramadje while waiting for the end of the cold season. I decided to stay in Gunnison to see if Tom's proposal worked. At the end of worship service, I reminded him of his proposal, and the following Sunday, he brought me the application form. I took it, and when I got home, I filled it out. I included the photos taken in Chad working as a nurse and mailed them to the address that was on the application form.

Toward the end of November, Prudy Mitchell, the director of nursing (DON) called me; as at that time, we were not working every day, I picked the date for my appointment. One of the employees drove me to SCC. The friend went for his errands and recommended that I should call him as soon as I finished with the interview. At the front desk, I asked to see the DON Prudy and Christina who worked there and took me to the office. Since it was a job interview, she called Marty to be with her. Seeing my application and the photos, the DON was touched.

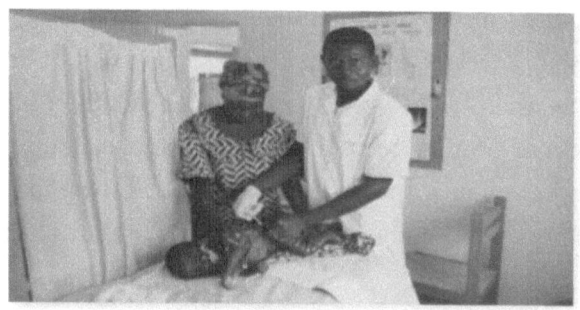

The problem right now was that the scheduling for the training would be in a few months. I assumed she had requested the activities position, but the answer was unsatisfactory.

She said, "I'm putting you on the floor as a nurse aide [NA] to wait for the training."

She made a tour of the center with me, and I was moved to see the older people in large numbers, which was rare in Chad. The tour was also an opportunity to introduce me to the administrator, Wade Baker; the nursing department staff, and other departments, such as culinary and activities. I told her that I could start on December 15, 2008. I thanked them, and I walked out happy and grateful to God for his blessings. My friend took me back to Almont. I told my boss Dan that I would not go to Castle Rock with him when our contract in the mountains ended. It was a bit of a shock, reading his face and seeing the change in attitude. I did not report, but when I was talking about my choice to stay in Gunnison, Gifford Jauregui wanted me to stay with his family, but Gary, my friend, who I said was also giving me a ride to church said that I should stay with him and his brother Glen. As a reader, you do not get the idea of this grace. (Gary's house was one block from SCC, but Gifford's house was going to require a daily ride to work.)

On December 6, 2008, I packed all my things, including the gifts I received on-site at Almont (the bed a client gave me and the bicycle Dan gave me). I missed the promise of the utensils because I quit before the scheduled date for the whole team to leave the house. But that was okay. Gifford and Gary loaded my stuff with me. When we finished loading, Gifford asked me to drive the truck, and he would be next to me to guide me. As soon as we entered Gunnison, he asked me to take another direction toward Gary's house to avoid crossing downtown, where there would be a lot of traffic and people. Luckily, we got safely to the house. Having my room cleaned, we got all the stuff out, and we placed them in my new room. It was another phase of my adventure.

BEGINNING OF LIFE IN GUNNISON

The first week was devoted to rest and to do my long-distance courses. I also took the opportunity to transfer my mailbox to Gunnison. On December 15, I introduced myself and started my orientation beside a former certified nurse assistant. I was kept in day shift for quite a while. Later, I also did the evening shift. I had only been following the schedule until January 2009.

Gunnison Times, which was Gunnison's local newspaper, wrote about me, and it made me a little more popular even though I was a newcomer in the Gunnison area.

By the middle of January, I was told that the training for nurse's assistants would be effective in February. Because of the three new hires, we had reached a number of four students in class. Fortunately for me, RN Vicky, who would be the teacher, spoke French because her husband was from France. The training was a bit hard because I tended to translate everything in my head into French to understand the lesson and the context of the questions before answering them. The training was from February 9 to February 23, 2009, then the training was over. It was Amy, Kevin Plowman, and I who had gone all the way, but our fourth colleague deserted. The steps were taken for our state test, and wisely, I chose the Colorado Springs site because Kevin had his family there and he was willing to give me ride and to stay at their house. We made the first trip so we could take the test the next day.

Staying at Kevin's mother's house, at night, I had a dream that we took the exam, but the administration told us that there were no results. I was confused, thinking about my failure or something like that. Who would bring me back? And where would I be staying if I had to take the exam a second time? These were questions that hovered in my head in the morning while forgetting my miracle-working God "who is the same yesterday today and forever" (Hebrews 13:8). In the morning, Kevin, seeing outside, noticed that there was a lot of snow on the ground. He told me that we had to hurry so we would not be late. We went to the testing center, and there were no cars in the parking lot. A note was posted at the door that the exam was canceled due to the snowstorm. The whole situation was the meaning of my nightly dream.

Without delay, we made our way back to Gunnison. Another appointment was made, and the exam took place on April 30, 2009. I passed the written test and skills, which were part of the exam. I was overwhelmed with joy because it was a breaking point, and it gave me the assurance of a job in Gunnison. I was grateful to Kevin for his kindness. The success helped increase my hourly wage. April was a month of joy because of this success, but sadness followed. Toward the end of May, precisely on May 22, 2009, they called from Chad to inform me of my father's death. It was not possible for me to travel. RMCM and some members of the church supported me financially. I added my savings and transferred the money to Chad. SCC gave me a day or two of mourning, and I went back to work.

Communication with people was my nightmare. Everyone who worked with me had difficulty understanding my so-called spoken English. I decided to sign up for the adult English language course.

Understanding that I would stay a long time, I wanted to apply for my family's immigration. I got the phone number of Ellen Peterson, who worked at human resources in Gunnison, from a woman in Crested Butte. I called Ellen, and she welcomed me at her office to fully understand my need. She told me that at their level, she did not deal with immigration matters, but Catholic Charities of the Diocese of Pueblo was the perfect place for my situation. She put me in contact with Adriana Fernandez, the coordinator, and the appointment was made for a first interview. I explained to the pastor, and he gave the church truck to Larry, my old friend from Almont, to drive me to Pueblo. Adriana explained the procedures and fees to me. I was happy and worried at the same time about the expense, thinking about the length of time I had to save the money for six people ($480 each). I left everything in God's hands. My major occupations were doing full-time CNA work, attending church, and learning English, which I mentioned before. In addition, I had registered for International TEFL Teacher Training (ITTT) to complete one hundred hours of lessons. Speaking of occupations, quite often, on Sundays, Gifford taught me how to drive.

I will mention an important meeting with special people. It happened according to God's plan in my life. Michelle Duft and her family got to know me at RMCM. At Christmas Eve in 2008, she invited me to attend the meeting organized by the New Song Church at Gunnison County Fairgrounds with them. As soon as we entered the room, the first people who greeted me asked me where I came from. Once they understood that I was from Chad immediately, they told me that I had to meet the couple Jack and Amy Perry because they had their daughter Julie Perry who had gone to Chad as a missionary. This first contact was an open door that allowed Julie to meet my family later.

Jack and Amy had arranged to meet with them, and they gave me an appointment for another contact because they were planning to go to Chad in 2009. We arranged a plan, as they were going to Chad to meet my family. Despite the absence of physical address, they were able to meet my family and see my newborn daughter Grace before me. Boyd Pederson and his father offered me a plane ticket through their earned miles, and for the allowance, it came from the money many other friends gave me to supplement my little savings, and I was able to travel to Chad in February 2010 to see my family again and to see my late father's grave.

As soon as I was back in Gunnison after one to two months, several volunteers decided to teach me how to drive, among them was Sean, a friend in town; Kevin Zimmermann, a colleague at work; and Angie and David Hammond, the friends who were the guests of Glen, whom I met at the house. During this time, I had been alerted to move because the two friendly brothers planned to do the same in the days to come. I was looking for listings of houses for rent. I was worried that I would not find a place near the nursing home. The snow season would make it difficult to ride the bike for a long distance due to the cold and risk of slipping. Luckily, I saw a room for rent in a *Gunnison Times* ad, and it was Mark Peterson who posted it, and he became my first official landlord. On April 1, 2010, Mary, her husband Scott, and Gary helped me move in with Mark, who lived a few blocks from the workplace.

The desire to be able to drive before the snow period grew more and more. Finally, there was a lady in town whose phone number I found on the internet and who taught people driving or taking the test. She found out that I had already mastered the steering wheel when I was driving with her, so she offered me her car for the test. By another grace of God, I passed my driving test on June 10, 2010. A month later, on July 11, 2010, after a worship service, I was chatting with Mrs. Sharalee Boyd about getting my driver's license. I mentioned the desire to get a car that would help me drive daily.

She said, "Nouba do you want a car? You know, Annie and Duncan were looking to offer their old Subaru model car to someone because they got a new car. Let us go talk to them now."

As we were chatting outside, we went back inside. After talking about the condition of the car, Duncan went home to bring me the title. I thanked them all and put my bike in the trunk of the Subaru and drove by myself for the first time. Sundays after getting my own car, alternately, Barb Malloy and Kay Rutherford voluntarily gave me gasoline money. This act of charity continued even when my family arrived later. We still received financial and material help from them. Another one-time surprise that I would never forget was the gift of money from Gabrielle Kellman. She was a student at WSCU doing her own business at the same time. As she was a Christian at RMCM. She understood that I was struggling to bring my family from Africa. She handed me an envelope saying that God had put in her heart to help me financially. Knowing her student status, I was surprised to see $600 in the envelope. I thanked her dearly, and she just said, "Don't mention. I just obey God."

Instead of working full time to earn more money, I decided to go to college. After my application, all the staff (studies and finances) were people who had a relationship with fellows I also knew. In terms of finances, Mr. Bill told me that the subsidized federal loan was enough to cover my tuition, as I was going to be external. It was a good idea not to get into more debt with the unsubsidized loan. Seeing that the amount of money would be enough for my Pueblo program, I told him to give some anyway. Having received the money, Adriana recommended that I made the money order for each member of the family and to take the money order back to Pueblo on my break time. This time, Tom Hart, my friend from church and now coworker, drove me to Pueblo to pay the costs. The university studies were a test, which was hard, but I made it with the support of Dan Parr, my classmate, and the other friends until I finished the academic year from August 2010 to May 2011.

As the same amount of loan was still given in the second semester, it had helped me go back to Chad for the second time in September 2011. I said September because in August 2011, I refused to reregister. The Pueblo process was moving forward, but I got stuck in a situation. My salary, according to the government, was not enough to feed six people plus myself in the United States. Adriana, with her assistant Viviana, advised me to find another sponsor; otherwise, the files would be blocked for a long time. If I spoke to the church about it, maybe a member would have signed up, but I decided to ask David Hammond, the friend I met at Gary's house, first. David responded positively.

He was told to send in his tax forms. He did it, and the two annual incomes (his and mine) were sufficient. I, by faith, reassured my friend David that my family would not be a burden to him. Signing up as a sponsor would involve expenses to feed, clothe, and house the beneficiaries, but I didn't think so because I relied on Philippians 4:19: "And my God shall supply all your need according to His rich in glory by Christ Jesus."

At the start of 2012, my coworker Jeanette Klepinger became the manager of Gunnison's food pantry. She asked me if I could help with the transport. The food bank received donations from City Market, Walmart, Safeway, and even from vendors, so the role of the carriers was to collect these donations, register them, and arrange them, if possible, depending on the location (perishable and nonperishable items). It was purely voluntary, but the manager gave me permission to take what I liked to eat because it was not all that was on the shelves that interested me. My food was ensured, so it was a plus, and I could save money for the situation of my family, who were looking for a way to come to the US.

My projects in the first semester of 2012 were to obtain a minibus for seven people, a house with at least three or four bedrooms, and financial support to finalize my family's visas in Yaoundé, Cameroon. Already, in February 2012, my family was supposed to go to Yaoundé. I spoke with Martha, whose name I mentioned being my colleague from Bible College. She was transferred to Yaoundé; as she understood that my family was going to join me, she was not worried about their number of seven people because my wife brought Lydie, our deaconess from the Church of Chad, to help take care of the five children. I sent the money for their transportation, food, and paperwork, as requested by the embassy. My family went to Cameroon. Who knew the length of their stay? It could be short or long. Finally, after four months of waiting, the embassy gave them the visas, and they left for N'Djamena. The cause of my family's long wait was the DNA procedure. Viviana's team in Pueblo who oversaw the dossiers told me that DNA was required to confirm that I am the biological father of all five children. Gunnison County Health, led by Carol, played an important role. They agreed to help me out. Sherry Dietz, the immunization lady, took my saliva to send to the testing center for free. On the children's side, I paid for each of them, and from Cameroon, they took their saliva samples as well. They were shipped to the same testing center here in the US. Once finished, the DNA proved that they were all my children; therefore, the visa process continued until the end.

For my part, I fought to prepare their arrival to the States by faith. In March 2012, I randomly shared with Wendy Stickler, another colleague, the desire to buy a house even if it were a mobile home to accommodate my family, who would arrive at any time from N'Djamena. She told me that besides the work at Senior Care Center, she also worked on mortgages, so she wanted to help me find a house. The salary and credit score checks were done, and she told me that I was qualified for an FHA loan. She told me to find a house and to inform her. Since I had Jack and Amy who had been residents of Gunnison for a long time, I asked them to search for the house with me. Jack told me that twenty years ago, Shirley Woodbury helped them buy their home, so he was going to contact her to help me as a buyer broker. To my surprise, Shirley was the mother-in-law of Jean W. Woodbury who was MDS at SCC. During our first interview with Shirley, she asked me $2,000 for the preliminary home purchase. Having made a lot of other expenses, I did not have this kind of money saved. I told Jack that if buying a house was impossible, my family and I could rent while waiting. Unanimously, Amy and Jack told me that they were going to lend me that money, and I would reimburse them according to my means until I would finish paying. I accepted the offer, and then I kept my promise and paid them back portion by portion, the whole amount, and they were proud of me. If I had borrowed from a bank, I would pay it back with huge interest. The house searches were done in town, and there was none that neared my mortgage loan amount. When Shirley searched in Antelope Hills, located ten miles from Gunnison, there were three choices. It looked like the two houses would give me trouble financially, but the one at 359 Mesa Loop was chosen. Shirley was well experienced with her job, and she got me a good deal. The closing formalities were carried out on May 4, 2012, and I was given the keys to my first house. Jack and Amy, with the help of the Christians from New Song Church, had come to dust and clean the house for me. Kelly Black, a Christian from RMCM, was also a nurse at SCC. She was moving during this period. She decided to give me her supplies (couch, table, chairs, and television). Jack and Matt carried the whole thing into the house. God helped me to get an all-furnished house before my family eventually would arrive.

A blessing came unexpectedly from my colleagues at my workplace. God was still doing a lot of things in March 2012. One night at the end of my shift, my Subaru did not start. My colleagues Kevin Zimmermann and Greer, who were boyfriend and girlfriend before separating later, noticed my trouble. They got out of their Toyota minivan and walked toward me. They asked me what was wrong. I told them my car would not start. Certainly, they agreed before approaching me. Kevin told me that he and Greer wanted to give me their minivan if I was okay with the offer. At first, it was a shock to me. I said yes. They told me that tomorrow, they would bring me the title, and as the car needed some repairs due to the accident they had, I had to put some money for the repair; nevertheless, it was drivable. The promise was kept, and I was in possession of a second car.

Gifford, my mechanic, advised me instead to exchange the minivan with a Suburban that did not require repair. I took the advice in consideration to avoid expenses that I did not know would be huge. Humans are humans; the Suburban did not please me and did not have enough seats for seven people. It was my turn to suggest to Gifford to sell the Suburban, and if I could complete it, buy the real minivan for my family. Things were done, and after a few days of negotiations made by Gifford in Grand Junction, my minivan had arrived in Gunnison.

All these efforts were not yet essential. What was important and crucial was to find the airline tickets for my family (six people in total). As usual, at RMCM, the opportunity was always given to anyone who wanted a prayer at the end of the service. It was in May; I was waiting for my turn to go and ask for a prayer. Pastor John Clement and Bonnie Thompson were the two intercessors that Sunday. As the pastor was still praying for someone and Bonnie was free, waiting for other people, I went to see her. I told her that my family got the visas, I had to bring them to the USA, but I did not have enough money for their plane tickets.

She said to me, "Let us pray for the miracle of God." She ardently interceded for the situation. At the end of her prayer, she added, "Nouba, we are going to do the yard sale for a fundraising called Family Reunion Fundraising." She said that she was going to let the pastor know about this plan that God had put in her heart. Next Sunday, the pastor expressed his agreement. The news was already circulating through the announcement made by Bonnie on the local *Gunnison Times* newspaper. The ad said that anyone who wanted to get rid of anything from their home had to take the things there to David and Bonnie Thompson's. At SCC, Kelly Black also informed the staff. Not only did the staff donated, but Beth, her sister Jacquie, and their friend Cara Faulds brought the effects of their mother, Ann Starrit, an SCC resident who loved me very much during her lifetime.

On my trip back from Chad, I showed her the photos of my family, and she said that she was going to kiss them at all costs before she died, but God took her back before their arrival. They even opened a bank account at Gunnison Savings and Loans on behalf of my family.

Even on the day of the yard sale, which was held in the courtyard of RMCM, people still brought a lot of things.

The buyers were numerous, and every person who asked for the price of this or that, the organizers told them that the sale was only by donation. People would take small or valuable things and gave what God put in their hearts. Lots of stuff were picked up or bought, but there was still so much left.

Stacia, who was counting the money, exclaimed, "Nouba, that was a miracle!" She said that she had never witnessed so much money in one day of a yard sale like that. Alan Marquez and Marilyn, ex-missionaries in Chad, who, through Michael Manitha, I was able to meet in Denver in 2009, also gave a large sum of money.

The missionary couple had the privilege of meeting my family on their trip to Chad while attending a church conference. Before this important financial aid for the reunification of my family, RMCM bought proclaimers (audio of New Testament in dialects) and, later, after the arrival of my family RMCM, sent a large sum of money for the roof of the church in Kamnda, for which I was the pastor before immigrating to the United States.

I will testify more about God's blessings before the arrival of my family. One day, I was walking toward the front door of City Market, and there was a curious lady talking to me. I told her my name and my country of origin. She said that she lived in Ethiopia for years in the past. She took my phone number, promising to invite me to her house one day. It was Maureen O'Donnel, who had become friends with the Baroumbaye family until now. She was the provider of clothes, shoes, and other items to each member of my family.

Another generous couple that I had met was when I was at Safeway; I was able to buy whatever I wanted, but I needed something else, but I did not know the name. I had bagels at home; at least I was able to know the name of this quality of bread, which I learned from the food pantry. I saw a lady in the aisle.

I told her, "Ma'am, I have bagels at home, but I do not have what I am supposed to put in it before eating."

She said, "Let's go see if we can find any cream cheese."

She showed me the cream cheese, and I took a box of it. Before letting me go, she asked me, as it is usual here in the USA, "Where are you from?"

She was not the first person to ask this question. This time, I thought to myself, *Is this question to know where I came from originally or who was this foreigner who did not know cream cheese?* She told me her name, which was Catherine Nance, and that she lived with her husband, Joe, here in Gunnison.

She added that if I was not too busy every day, she wanted my service to go to their house and cut the grass in their yard. I agreed, the appointment was made, and I was able to carry out the project. Catherine and her husband were satisfied with my work. Madame paid me, and she told me that she had something for me if I could accept. One of her neighbors had passed away, and she wanted to bring me into the house if I wanted some necessary things for my family that would come soon. We went there, and indeed, I found things that we could use. This acceptance motivated her later to take us to another home with my family, and we benefited from many other things that were going to be donated to Goodwill. Catherine and Joe kept a good relationship with us until we moved to Grand Junction.

Jack and Amy played a very important role in the education of my children. They initiated the meeting with Jackie Burt, the director of One Room School (ORSCH), to talk to me about the advantage that my children would have by going to this school, as they had no background in English. Grace, the youngest, had not yet gone to school in Chad, but the four had gone to learn French, except Sephora, the oldest, who learned basic English at the beginning of high school. By their effort, they got the scholarship from ACE. This initiative helped the four children throughout the school year, but the youngest had to finish her school year at the kindergarten ran by Nancy. There would still be a lot of such testimony in the lines to come, but let us talk about the family journey first.

THE FAMILY'S TRIP FROM CHAD TO GUNNISON, COLORADO

Contributions from all over were enough to pay for the airline tickets of my six family members. A lot of suggestions had been made to me by people. For example, looking for guides who would take care of my family from Chad to the destination or going myself and bringing them back. I obeyed God's guidance, which was to "pay the airline tickets and let God guide your wife and the children." I did not know the connection system, so instead of choosing the airport in Washington, DC, which would be the entry airport and at the same time the connection point for Denver International Airport (DIA), I made a mistake, thinking that I was smart. The arrival should be at Dulles, but the connection should be from Ronald Reagan Airport for DIA. I was happy because it saved me a few bucks, compared to connecting from Dulles, according to research done online on the day of booking. I had my minivan but had never driven to Denver and back on my own, so I was afraid to try not to endanger the entire family life. Driving inside of Denver itself would be a big problem as well. Pastor Chris from New Song Church offered me the minivan that I just had to pay for gasoline, but I refused for the same reasons.

The day of departure for the family from Chad was August 5, 2012, and with the time zone difference, they were due to arrive in Washington on August 6. I informed Ramadje and his parents, Moukobaye and

Zara, of my arrival and the probable arrival of the family in Denver. Alan's family was also informed. Alan was still working at the airport. He made a proposal that came from God's plan and favor for me and my family. Although working at the airport, he was on the maintenance side, but he had friends who could lead the family step-by-step until outside the airport. He did not stop there. He added by saying that my family would spend the night at his place, and that in the morning, Marilyn, his wife; he; and his son Jonathan; his wife; and their baby would bring us to Gunnison. Early in the morning of August 5, 2012, I traveled by bus to Denver. I did not want to risk anything; therefore, I avoided traveling on the same day, August 6. Being in Denver, I spoke with Alan about my arrival and the approximate time of the family's arrival; however, Alan's mind was already prepared for the schedule. Before leaving Gunnison, Catherine told me that she was going to cook dinner for my guests.

In the middle of the day on August 6, I received a phone call. It was an agent from Dulles Airport who told me that my wife wanted to talk to me. We were overwhelmed with joy (Moukobaye, Florence's older brother; his wife, Zara; and me). The purpose of the call was not just to announce their arrival but to tell me that the people at the airport were asking her to pay for their bus transportation from Dulles Airport to Ronald Reagan Airport. I told Florence to hand the phone to the person. Without arguing, I paid the amount with my credit card. Getting to the next airport was not easy, but with the help of the right people, they made it to Ronald Reagan Airport. Another phone call came to us. This time, it was to pay for the luggage as the luggage prices were not included in the ticket from Washington, DC, to Denver International Airport (DIA).

In the same way, I still paid over the phone with my credit card. After the conversation, there was no way to communicate because she did not have the phone. What we knew was that they had to stop in Atlanta, Georgia, before coming to Denver. Thinking of saving dollars when booking airline tickets, I was wrong with all the last-minute expenses. Proverbs 3:5–6 says, "Trust in Lord with all your heart and lean not on your own understanding. In all your ways acknowledge Him, and He shall direct your paths."

During the evening, seeing the arrival time approaching, we went to the airport but first to Alan's workplace to follow his instructions. The plan was to stay outside of the airport and wait. Alan and his friend inside the airport would take them to us. With eyes on the exit door, Madame and the children were exiting, being led by Alan. I was very excited to kiss them, but Alan said we had to hurry because we might have problems with the police. We took off in the direction of Alan's house. They were tired, the meal Alan and his family had offered was not to the children's taste, especially the pizza, which was a whole new menu for them.

To remember Chad, Alan brought out the cassettes of songs in Sara from Chad, and it was a real party (dance and songs mixed). There was Alan's children, their family, those of the house, my basketball team (seven members of my family), Ramadje, and his parents altogether. Unbelievable, but the house was full that night. I called Jack and Amy but also Bonnie to confirm the safe arrival of the family. Bonnie wanted to meet them the same day when we would arrive to Gunnison. Jack and Amy, on the other hand, said that the guests should have dinner at their place before going home. Catherine, the friend I met while looking for cream cheese at Safeway, and her husband Joe said they would bring dinner for the guests as well. I immediately shared all this information with Alan to prepare their mind about Gunnison's program upon arrival. The hosts showed us the rooms to spend the night. In the morning, songs on cassettes resounded in the living room. My family still felt like themselves in Chad with all these memories. Breakfast was offered plentifully. Sometime later, the luggage was loaded and prayer was pronounced for our protection; we embarked and departed from Thornton. The plan was to stop in Denver, say goodbye to Ramadje's parents, then go to his workplace to get the fridge he gave me to replace mine, which was small and old. After loading the fridge, they took us somewhere for lunch. After the meal, it was finally our effective departure toward Gunnison. The children, still tired, were getting enough sleep. We stopped when we needed to go to the bathroom.

As it was August, it was not yet dark outside when we arrived at the courtyard at RMCM Church in Gunnison. We stopped to allow Bonnie and other available church women to meet my family. As they already met them, we continued to Jack and Amy's to eat. After dinner, we came home. Catherine's meal awaited us. Not everyone ate because some were full. Despite the fatigue, we managed to fit the new fridge at its place. I thought of making the children sleep in the living room and giving the two bedrooms—one to the couple (Alan and Marilyn) and the other to Jonathan, his wife, and their baby. Alan was telling me that they had booked a motel, so they were going to leave us and go to sleep. As they were to leave immediately for Thornton in the morning, this same evening, they said their goodbye to us until the next reunion.

Family life started on August 8, 2012. The family was made up of myself; my wife, Florence; my fourteen-year-old daughter, Sephora;

my eleven-year-old son, Kelita; my nine-year-old daughter, Mathilde; my seven-year-old son, Daniel; and my four-year-old daughter, Grace.

After two days of rest, I returned to work. We went to town, to the grocery store, and to church; and I was everyone's interpreter, except to my wife and Sephora, who tinkered around a bit in English. From a schooling point of view, as everything was arranged by Jack, Amy, and Jackie Burt, the children were accepted into ORSCH. The transport problem arose. I was able to drop them off at school in the morning. At the end of school, I was still at my evening shift work. People of good will, that I hesitate to name them for fear of forgetting someone, gave rides home to my children during the whole school year because my wife was not yet driving.

As I mentioned before, the youngest, Grace, ended up with Nancy, who ran the kindergarten in town. The others, after this 2012–2013 school year, continued in public school according to their level. Dad the interpreter finally became a beginner in English compared to the children who had arrived without English vocabulary. Unfortunately, the little ones forgot Sara over the advantage of English as they came to the age of four and seven years old. Help was pouring in and school supplies were provided (Mark, Joe, and Catherine were part of this blessing). Clothing was provided by church members, like Kay Rutherford and others. But most of the clothes and shoes were donated through Maureen's charitable organization. My landlord, Mark, was a friend of the couple Deryl and Ann. Paintings were donated by Ann. Not only the paintings, but we got other things, such as a woodstove and firewood. Repairs at an affordable cost for the house were by Deryl.

My friendship with Deryl and Ann gave me the opportunity to ride a horse in the US. That was the one time I rode, and I did not have any other occasion until today.

The firewood was also provided by Denis Apsey; Matt, our neighbor, and his family; Ken and Becky; and Malloy. For two years receiving firewood, the load was not finished until we moved to Grand Junction in 2018. The food pantry blessed us with food continuously. Even during the change of managers, such as Joe and Katie Dix, replacing Jeannette Keplinger; and, later, Angie took their place.

For transportation, after the Subaru and Toyota minivan offered by Annie and Duncan, and Kevin and Greer, Tim Rutherford, through his neighbor, gave us a vehicle; in 2017, a nice woman gave us a car, Buick model, and Jeannette gave us her car, which lasted until 2020 before being destroyed in an accident. It is my pleasure to mention in this book our African friends (Ayo, Ola, their two boys, and Francis). They would come to the house, and as we all went to Rocky Mountain Christian Ministries, we often had the opportunity to stay together.

I will not ignore this lesson learned in family life. I wanted Florence and the kids to do things like me when I was alone. No clothes on the floor, no utensils in the sink, and lots of other rules that I had established. Each time, I scolded them. My wife did not do the same things the kids did, but sometimes, I raised my voice when talking to her even though I knew she was allergic to yelling. My point was that my attitude as grumpy dad and husband was contradicted. Every time people from everywhere told them that I was a good guy, they said that I was a good guy outside but not with them at home. After several years, God gave me the grace to be tolerant, patient, and calm.

In May or June 2013, my wife, Florence, started working at the Water Wheel Inn Hotel. It did not last because of the hotel's downtime. Around October, she was forced to change jobs, and she joined Sodexo, the cafeteria of Western State Colorado University (WSCU). The Baroumbaye family were grateful to Becky Glover and Jon Coady, who made this permanent work opportunity possible. Later, Madame tried to change to another job at our nursing home, but it was an adventure, and she decided to go back to Sodexo, where she stayed until we moved to Grand Junction.

I was supposed to take my US citizenship test in 2013, after five years, but the circumstances caused some delay, and I took it in 2015, and I passed the test, which favored my children, who were all under the age of eighteen, to become US citizens. My wife took her test at the end of 2018 in Denver and had participated in an oath-taking ceremony with other candidates in Grand Junction in the beginning of 2019.

I tried to do the Organo Gold coffee business in 2014 because of the motivation of Chadian friends (Samuel Mbainayel and Jean Nengondingam), and that was an adventure. The manager of Allsports Replay authorized me to set up my coffee table by his bike shop. The trial did not last because of the cold spell. I asked the businessmen downtown to give me space to sell my coffee but with no satisfactory result.

Finally, my barber Kevin Coblentz said yes to my request, and I used a corner of his barber shop for my sale. A few customers bought it but not enough for a good business project. He and his friend advised me to go out from time to time in other shops with hot water in a thermos, as my coffee was instant; those who were interested could buy it. Many shop managers were adamant: "No soliciting." The effort was not successful. The discouragement was beginning to take ahold of me.

Winter was coming to its end, and I decided to thank Kevin and shut down the business at the barber shop. Some people were interested in the quality of the coffee, and they continued ordering it whenever their supplies ran out. My failure in this business made me think again about studying. I enrolled at the Community College of Denver (CCD) to study business. Classes had to be online because I lived in Gunnison, and the college was in Denver. The computer I had was not working well, but Robert gave me one that worked. Whenever I had a problem, I would bring it back, and he would fix it for me for free. Ann and Robert were also good friends in Gunnison. They also supplied us a lot with produce from their garden. I was very grateful to the managers of the Gunnison Public Library while studying online, for allowing me to do proctored testing in their premise. With the help of God, I finished my studies for the associate degree in business in May 2017. The diploma was to try to restart another business, but which one? No idea had come up.

At the end of 2017, new thoughts animated me. I told myself that I would risk starting to pay back my federal loan for the degrees that I would never use if I lived in Gunnison. I thought about moving with my family and going to Denver if I could do the nursing program. I applied for the mortgage, and I was eligible. My condition of carrying out the house search was linked to obtaining a permanent job as a CNA either at the hospital or at the nursing home. No employer responded. Tired of waiting, I said living in Grand Junction had to be the second option because Colorado Mesa University had an excellent nursing program too. Continuing to pray for divine guidance, I applied to two hospitals (Community Hospital and Saint Mary's Hospital) and a nursing home (Genesis Mesa Manor). By faith, I also changed the Denver loan officer with Ashley who was working at Grand Junction Fairway mortgage company, and she found for us the buyer broker Sara. We made a couple of trips to inspect the first homes she offered. None were satisfactory, so we went back to Gunnison, and I was telling Florence that we would risk renting rather than buying a house.

When my loan officer heard this, she said to me, "With the number of people you had in your household, it was better to buy than to rent a house."

It was truly a commendable idea, and I had not regretted accepting it. I did my own research and found the house online at 671 Faircloud Way, Grand Junction, CO 81504. The buyer broker appreciated my choice. The real steps began without any doubt or hesitation. In early February 2018, Community Hospital and Genesis both responded and asked me to come in for the interview on a date of my choice. I chose the same date but different times. My wife decided to come with me.

My first interview was with Community, as it was in my human wisdom that I wanted to work there to benefit from my hospital experience. At the end of the interview, the staff who welcomed me told me that they would call me afterward to tell me the result. We rushed for the other interview at Genesis. Officials Paul, Brenda, TJ, and Lorretta were at the interview. I answered their questions, and at the end, they asked me when I wanted to start working. I told them that I had to respect the fifteen days of resignation notice according to the job rule. Very happy, my wife and I left for Gunnison, and the next day, I officially deposited my notice to quit the job. I communicated to the HR of Genesis the date of March 1, 2018, as the first day to start at their facility. The people of SCC (staff and residents were at the same time happy for my nursing program project and sad for my quitting plan). A big farewell party was offered to me in recognition of the good collaboration in the work for almost a decade (December 2008 until the end of February 2018).

Robert: During the party for goodbye, he said "when you get your nursing license come back here"

Ex-Administrator Wade Baker: Let us get started here-this is an easiest invitation-Nine years ago- a young man came to Gunnison from Africa. Couple years later he was able to bring his family- I was administrator- you work here as a CNA and you have done it so well- as Robert said if you go and get your nursing degree, you are welcome to come back- we build you a new building (Audience laughed)- nine years you did a wonderful service to our residents-Thank you Nouba! Loud acclamation!

Ex Director of Nursing Prudy Mitchell: When Nouba came to the job interview with me in December- he sent the application and I call him for the interview- I just want to express to you what happened to me that day-closed my door after our appointment I got on my knees and I just sobbed, I really did, because I have never met in my entire life somebody so humble and - indeed we had been recipients at this nursing home facility. All of us not only resident and stage, families and our wonderful vendors, noun we can't thank you enough for coming to minister to us- you were an unbelievable mentor to all of us, supervision and manager we learned so much from you-your dedication your love you mercy help a lot in our business, We wish well-success, you and your family-I know this is hard for you because you are quite part of our family, but there gonna be so many out there to benefit in their organization -if god wants it you will be back with us too much joy too much happiness- we wish you well-love you- we can't thank you enough as I said.

She finished by the song: For he is a jolly good fellow (x3) which nobody can deny.

The CEO Robert, Human Resources Director Christina, ex-administrator Wade Baker, and ex-director of nursing Prudy Mitchell were present, along with other staff members. Many thanks to Andrea, Tyler, and others who were the main organizers. At the end of the party, I said goodbye to everyone and left the building with gifts and the promise made by the organizing team to send me more in the days to come, and they did indeed keep their promise. Speaking of gifts received, they were countless, like the stereo given by Jim and Missy, not to forget Jim's mom, who loved me very much until her death. Beth and Jacquie bought me a video camera and another family gave me a camera; these effects still exist as a commemoration.

On February 28, 2018, I left Gunnison to come to Grand Junction. As I booked my stay at the Travelodge Hotel for thirteen days, I moved there to start working on March 1, 2018. After a few days of orientation with a former certified nurse assistant (CNA), Eva, I was starting to master the routine. I would come back to Gunnison on weekends because I missed my family and church. The steps to complete the home purchase had accelerated but with some last-minute surprises. The loan officer was asking me for more than $5,000 out of pocket. I did not have the amount, but luckily, a nice gentleman from Grand Junction and the couple Jack and Amy from Gunnison lent me their money. March 13, 2018, was maintained for the closing. Another surprise occurred on March 12. The loan officer told me that the underwriter, when finalizing the accounts, said that I had to bring $3,000 in the form of money order on the day of closing. It was a dilemma, as I was at the end of my hotel stay, hoping to sleep in my house the next day, and suddenly, I was asked not $300 but $3,000. The loan officer advised us to borrow the money from the payday loan. She asked and was told that they could not lend more than $1,000. I made some phone calls to some people, but they told me that they did not have the amount of money requested. My wife and I went to our bank (Bank of the West). The Grand Junction branch manager said he should contact the Gunnison branch to give us the answer. After his contact, he came back to say his apologies because Gunnison branch said no to the loan.

Confidently, I said to the manager, "Don't apologize, our God will give us the $3,000 for the closing today."

My confidence was based on Hebrews 11:1: "Now faith is the substance of things hoped for, the evidence of things not seen." We left the bank with the idea of going to a restaurant to get something to eat. After I parked, I told my wife, "I am going to call Gifford from Gunnison."

As the phone rang, Gifford answered and told me he was driving out of state. Without delay, I had gone straight to the point: "I need $3,000 today for the closing of our house and that I will pay you back as soon as I have the expected money in a week."

He replied, "I'm going to call Elaina, my wife. She will call you. Then tell her how you want to receive the money."

I thanked him and let him continue his journey. I instructed Elaina to transfer the $3,000 to my account. We went in another Grand Junction branch to withdraw it in the form of money order before the time indicated for the closing. The loan officer called to check if I got the money, so with dignity, I said yes, and she said, "See you soon."

The closing took place, and as all my belongings were in my car, hoping not to go back to the hotel, we came directly to the house to officially spend our first night on March 13, 2018. Within a short period of time, I reimbursed all the loans required on the closing eve and the previous ones. What a miracle that during the first half of March 2018, work and house were acquired by the grace of God. The rest of March and the beginning of April, I continued to visit my family and attend worship service in Gunnison.

As our plan was to move the rest of the family in June, I started looking online for a local place of worship. I saw several churches, but my attention fell on Faith Heights Church (FHC) led by John and Carla Cappetto. I clicked on a video, and it was a lady named Kandace Peterhans giving her testimony to invite people to church. She said the empty chair was for anyone who heard her testimony. The spirit told me it would be me who would occupy the empty chair. I told Florence that I was going to attend the worship service at FHC because the Lord led me there. She and the children took advantage of the weekend to come and taste the atmosphere of worship by comparing with RMCM of Gunnison. They appreciated it, but the difference was the number of Christians at FHC that exceeded that of RMCM. I resumed my role of usher sometime after I joined the church. This church applied what was said in Leviticus 25:35 (NIV): "If one of your brethren becomes poor and falls into poverty among you, then you shall help him, like a stranger or a sojourner, that he may live with you."

Later, the eight months of nursing program was not easy. My mortgage payment was threatened because I was working fewer hours. One Sunday after the service, Pastor John Cappetto asked us how we were doing during COVID-19. We told him about the mortgage payment delay, and he said he needed to speak with his team to help us. When we got home, his assistant Dominic informed us over the phone that we had received a donation of $500, which was to go toward the mortgage. We gave him the contact, and the payment was made on their side to our mortgage company. We received the payment of the Valentine's ceremony from Sara, the responsible for the children at FHC. On the Christmas of 2020, the beloved Galleo told us that he and his wife had a gift for the Baroumbaye family. When we opened the envelope that he brought, it was $300. We have lived miracles after miracles attending FHC on top of all the lifesaving teachings from preachers.

One thing I did not mention about moving was that Sephora, our oldest daughter, tasted her freedom living alone a year before my Grand Junction project. As she wanted to do the nursing program, I suggested that she could enroll at Colorado Mesa University (CMU), but she refused, arguing that she was going to finish her four years at Western State Colorado University (WSCU). She added that she would stay at the university dorm. Her younger brother Kelita, who was going to be a senior at high school, wanted to stay in Gunnison because his track coaches did not want to lose him. Witnessing his repeated success in competitions, WSCU was planning to have him in their team so that he could compete at the college level. As there was no high school dormitory, Jack and Amy, together with Roy and Bev Duncan, suggested this idea to us. They said that Roy and Bev volunteered to host Kelita for a school year. We saw it as a miracle from God; therefore, Kelita finished the 2018–2019 school year by staying with them in the house until his graduation. The two couples put the height to their gratitude by organizing a big party during his high school graduation. During the holidays before the 2018–2019 academic year, Nanette Knuth, a Christian from RMCM, welcomed Kelita to stay in one of her rooms until he had access to the WSCU dormitory.

In June 2018, the Baroumbaye family was reduced to five members in the new home in Grand Junction. The Gunnison house could not remain vacant. Ryan Jordi, the realtor, tried to help us buy a house in Gunnison after my Denver attempt, but that also failed, then I turned to Grand Junction to finalize my move plan. To benefit concretely from his service, I entrusted him with the management of the house for rent. Quickly, he found tenants, warning them that they would stay for a short time if someone bought the house, but they could stay longer if the sale were delayed. Finally, the renting was short-term because at the beginning of 2019, a lady had closed on the house and became the owner of 359 Mesa Loop property.

The summer of 2018 was over, and as the steps to integrate Sodexo in Grand Junction had been completed, Florence, my wife, resumed her work at the beginning of the academic year at CMU. For my three children, Mathilde was enrolled at Central High School (CHS), Daniel was enrolled in Bookcliff Middle School, and Grace, being still in elementary level, had been enrolled in Thunder Mountain Elementary School. To come back to my case, as soon as the registration for CMU started, I had registered for a major in LPN-BSN. Confirmation letters started coming to my mailbox.

After attending a meeting of new students, at the same time, I did my orientation and registered for the required courses for the first semester from August to December 2018. As I transferred many of my previous credits, my prerequisites would only take two semesters. The lessons had to be in class, and I also worked full time, so it was not easy. I finished the first semester with a passing GPA in each lesson and even the lab, so I did not have to retake any course. During the holidays, an email was sent to students for whomever was interested in the healthcare program. The course was therefore titled Introduction to Health Care and would be taught by Renae Phillips, who became an asset for my admission to the nursing program. I was interested in this course, believing it would be a good opportunity.

When I linked it to the number of credits, I had to take it in my second semester; therefore, it had disrupted my schedule for transporting my children to school and for work. I tried to endure because to finish in good conditions, I would have the possibility of applying straightforwardly for the program and to start with the others in the academic year 2019–2020. Registration for nursing began before the end of the academic year. I did so, and later, I received the letter of admission with the condition of finishing the current classes with a C or better. After the admission letter, I was required to be interviewed to confirm my final position. On the day of my interview, three female managers were present. They were Gennell Stites, Tedra Gummin, and Linda Pilcher. In turn, they asked me questions. I answered them while apologizing for my remarkable accent, which made my conversation difficult. All of them encouraged me instead and said that they understood me fine.

One of the questions toward the end was this: "Why do you think you deserve to be selected for the nursing program?"

I replied, "Please take me because I will be a very good nurse the same way I was a nurse assistant."

Gennell told me, "It's true, we know you will be a good nurse." Proverbs 27:2 tells us this: "Let another man praise you, and not your own mouth; a stranger, and not your own lips." But as a reader of the Bible, I cannot base on a single verse to not speak of who I am. There was no sense of pride when Paul said in 1 Corinthians 14:18, "I thank

God I speak with tongues more than you all; yet in church I would rather speak five words with my understanding, that I may teach others also, than ten thousand words in a tongue." This is to say that there are many scriptures where people in the Bible can speak for themselves.

The rest of the time, before the end of the academic year, we were asked to submit all the required tests (background check, drug test, etc.). Everything seemed like I was ready for nursing, then in human wisdom, I planned a trip to Chad, which was to be made with my wife, Florence. The purpose of the trip was to visit the family and, more particularly, to see my younger brother gendarme Noubadoum Baroumbaye, who was suffering from brain cancer. Airline tickets were purchased in advance, awaiting the scheduled departure date in June 2019. Wisely, I went to the office to make sure all files were complete. Ronna Lee Sharpe (professional staff assistant) told me that everything was normal from the point of view of the documents to be submitted, but that academically, there were problems. She told me that I had a D in Anatomy Physiology II Lab (AP II Lab). Her kind answer was to call Genell Stites (PN coordinator and associate professor of nursing) to discuss my case and inform her of my plans to travel to Chad. Genell's response was inescapable: validate the AP II Lab or be excluded from the nursing program and reapply next year after validation. Ronna wanted my response immediately to either keep my name or cross me out and be replaced by whomever on the waiting list. She told me that the summer class for AP II Lab would start in two days, and since the professor had not yet closed the student list, I could contact her the same day to register and start with the others. It was a decision that did not even require consultation with my wife. For it was life or death matter. I said yes, and I would validate the course. Ronna gave me all the professor's information, and she called her too when I left the office.

When I arrived, the teacher told me that Ronna spoke with her about me. I checked in and took the schedule. It was when I got home that I explained everything to Florence. The refund of my airline ticket was not total, but the other side benefit was more important. This summer class was accelerated, and I finished with a grade of A. This success was the only condition I expected to keep my place in the nursing program. The academic year started in August 2019; it was difficult, but I finished the first semester well in December 2019. My younger brother's illness worsened, and he passed away in November. It was necessary to go to see the tomb in order to comfort myself because the circumstances prevented me from seeing him in his sufferings. My wife decided to accompany me. She paid for her plane ticket, but mine was offered by Genesis Employee Foundation (GEF). Big thanks to Merceydes Moffat (ex infection control director) and Deborah Mahrlig (GEF executive director) who made this offer possible.

February 26, 2020

After sending money to his family to assist with his brother's medical bills and funeral expenses, when his brother unexpectedly passed away, Nouba, a CNA at our Mesa Manor Center in CO, did not have any remaining funds to travel to attend his brother's memorial service in Chad, Africa. That's where our Genesis Employee Foundation (GEF) stepped in. GEF was able to assist Nouba, also a full-time nursing student and sole provider for his wife and five children, with his travel expenses.

We are truly thankful for all our employees who make the Genesis Employee Foundation possible. We care deeply.

It was then that we traveled at the end of December and returned to the United States in early January, shortly before the resumption of classes. Classes began in two months, and the global COVID-19 pandemic threatened the United States. All our clinical schedules in healthcare centers were canceled and were replaced by virtual clinical; also, our courses were online until the end of the academic year. The pinning and the graduation ceremony for many of our colleagues were both virtual, but some of us who did the virtual pinning had instead chosen to participate the graduation ceremony in person in August 2020.

My God is alive, and I used to say, "God is good all the time and all the time God is good." In May, the courses were over, and the pinning was done, which meant that we were officially trained nurses, but according to American law, we must first pass the National Council Licensure Examination (NCLEX) test before practicing in a healthcare institution. The testimonies about this test were always scary, and to prepare myself well, I had to pay Hurst Review Services to follow their training focused on the best way to take and to pass the NCLEX for the first time. God had opened other opportunities. My colleague Alyssa, who was also a new graduate, took advantage of the favor the State of Colorado had offered by allowing the graduates to use the temporary diploma acquired only by application. She did it and started working as a nurse. She advised me to do the same to have more money to pay for the NCLEX test fees. I shared the idea with my family and friends (Jack, Amy, and Julie, their daughter).

Without expecting anything other than working to pay the NCLEX fees that awaited me, my friends, the trio Jack-Amy-Julie, surprised me by sending me enough money to pay for the NCLEX. This coincidence motivated me to do both things at the same time—the application for the temporary diploma and that of the NCLEX test. The other graduates who paid for the test before me received their schedules two or three months later. At the end of June, during my application for the test, I expected to see my schedule around August or September, but to my surprise, the date of July 14 was available. I immediately reserved my position. July 14 was supposed to be my wife's birthday, and I had to take time off to go to Denver the day before. I told her that I had no other choice, and I chose July 14 for my NCLEX test, and I was confident that the result would be her unforgettable birthday present. At the beginning of July, I requested my days off and made the reservation in a hotel near the examination center. As a Christian, it was not only needed to intellectually and financially prepare for the test but also spiritually (fasting and prayer).

On July 13 in the morning, I left Grand Junction to go to Denver. I went directly to the hotel to confirm my presence. I had gone out to locate the examination center before coming back to rest. I refused to read my lessons but only read my Bible. My appointment was supposed to be at twelve o'clock, so my plan was to finish the exam and get back to Grand Junction at night. On July 14, around 9:00 a.m., I left the hotel to go to the examination center. As the examiners saw me arriving early, I thought they were going to tell me to wait for my scheduled time, but they just asked me to go through the access procedures. The check-in had been done, and they guided me to my spot and reminded me again of the actions to be taken as needed. They told me that I deserved the breaks if I wanted to take it during the exam. The system would alert me on my screen.

As soon as I clicked on the start button, I was concentrating on the exam, and I did not pay attention to the two periods of break offered because I did not want to waste a minute of my limited time. The last answer once given, the computer presented the survey to be taken, and that was the end of the exam. I collected my items and got out of the exam center. I called my wife to announce to her that I finished earlier than planned. In my car, my mind tried to think about the questions and their responses, but I resisted these thoughts each time they came back throughout the journey. I arrived safely in Grand Junction; therefore, I stopped at the City Market to buy a birthday cake for my wife. While we were sharing the cake, Florence asked me how I did in the test. I told her that the exam was totally different from the ordinary test or homework, but I kept the faith because I prayed to God a lot for that.

As a human, I let social media intimidate me. The other colleagues who composed before me posted their results and the very short time used during the exam (sixty minutes or ninety minutes) three or four days after the exam date. I checked my result every day, and I did not see anything. What appeared to DORA was only my temporary practical nurse (TPN). What I wanted to see was the practical nurse (PN). In almost a week, I received the email from the National Council of State Boards of Nursing (NCSBN), which reported my unofficial result, but the DORA site needed to confirm. I was scared because one of my teachers told me that a BSN level student received an email after her exam, but later, she found out that she failed. A colleague, out of curiosity, asked me if I had included the Department of Regulatory Agency (DORA) fee when I applied for the exam. I told her no, and she told me that unless I paid it, DORA would not confirm my admission to the official list. Without delay, I paid the fee, and the next day, my name officially appeared. I printed a copy and brought it to my workplace HR. My family, friends, and staff at Mesa Manor were all proud of me. There were no hours available to perform in my new position as an LPN, so I chose to work as CNA and worked as LPN on days when there was a shortage of nurses. This alternative did not last, as I got a full-time position and even overtime.

In June 2021, by the time I was finishing my draft book, my wife, Florence, continued to work at the cafeteria of Colorado Mesa

University (CMU). Sephora was engaged with Mamadou L. Kamara and was about to start the nursing program in Denver. Kelita had finished his sophomore year at Western State Colorado University (WSCU), Mathilde had graduated from Central High School, Daniel had finished his sophomore year at Central High School, and Grace had finished her seventh grade at Bookcliff Middle School.

This book was written to relate my journey so that my children can know how they arrived in the United States. This is not just to my offspring but to anyone who wants to know my story. It was also an opportunity to express my gratitude to everyone who, in one way or another, had contributed to the evolution of my course in life. While reading this book, someone would think that I forgot his or her good deeds. Please forgive me because it is hard to remember all the people and the good they had done in my life. May God help you to thank him and be satisfied for what he has done in your life.

REFERENCES

Burkhart, Michelle. "Stepping Back to 'Make a Life'." Gunnison Times, Gunnison Country Times, 29 Jan. 2009, www.gunnisontimes.com/.

Munroe, M. (2011). Understanding your place in God's Kingdom (p. 25) [Review of Understanding your place in God's Kingdom]. Destiny Image, Publishers, Inc.

All Scripture references from (The Holy Bible NKJV)
New King James Version
Copyright © 2013 by Holman Bible Publishers
Nashville, Tennessee 37234. All Rights Reserved
The Holy Bible, New King James Version
Copyright © 1982 by Thomas Nelson, Inc.

United States Department of State Washington D.C. 20520. (2006, October 1). Letter to Diversity Visa Applicants - 2007. U.S. Department of Labor Seal. http://www.doleta.gov/programs/onet/.)

ABOUT THE AUTHOR

Noubaissem Baroumbaye is the third child and first boy out of nine children in his family. He is married with Florence, and they have five children: three girls (Sephora, Mathilde, and Grace) and two boys (Kelita and Daniel). He is a Christian, and his caring gift made him work a lot in churches and in the healthcare system in Chad, Africa, and in the USA. It was not an ambition but a personal choice to write a book relating his story, which is full of gratitude expressed toward God and the people. Lessons about patience or perseverance are life savings that may help someone save his or her relationship and fulfill his or her dreams.